Tempus ORAL HISTORY *Series*

Bensham
Voices

Tempus ORAL HISTORY *Series*

Bensham
Voices

Pauline Groundwater

TEMPUS

Acknowledgements

My thanks go to all the people who have shared their memories and photographs for inclusion in this book, and for the many cups of tea and all the biscuits that were also shared during our chats.

The book would have been impossible without the input from my husband Ken, who shared interviews and did all the hard work bashing away at the computer keyboard. He was also my inspiration, and this book is dedicated to Ken and our family.

A special thank you to Lawrie for agreeing to write the Foreword, despite his heavy commitments. I would also like to thank John Gibson, the *Evening Chronicle* sportswriter, who showed great interest in the book and who kindly revised his schedule in order to supply photographs.

Pauline Groundwater

First published 2003

Tempus Publishing Limited
The Mill, Brimscombe Port,
Stroud, Gloucestershire, GL5 2QG

British Library Cataloguing in Publication Data.
A catalogue record for this book is available from the British Library.

ISBN 0 7524 2863 2

Typesetting and origination by Tempus Publishing Limited
Printed in Great Britain by Midway Colour Print, Wiltshire

Contents

Introduction

I was born and bred in the middle of Bensham, in the midst of long rows of terraced flats and cobbled streets. I remember the warmth of the people and the warmth of the sun as it glowed red upon the bricks after a rain shower. To me this was security and beauty; security in the safety of such a close-knit community and loving family, and beauty in these sunsets, which mellowed the grey streets with an autumn tinge.

As a child there was colour to be found everywhere in those steep streets. Not only colour but smells; the smell of the steam engines as they snorted their way along the main line at the bottom of the streets; the smell of the hops from the breweries that drifted across the river; the sulphur smell from the coke works at Norwood, and the mouth-watering smell from the fish and chip shops at the top of the street.

There was also so much kindness to be found there; some neighbours would draw you into their own family circle and take you to the park or seaside and treat you as one of their own, and other neighbours would be there to give support if anyone was ill.

Front doors were never locked – it was thought an insult to do so (except at night). There was also poverty to be found in those same streets, and despair in trying to make ends meet until the next wage packet arrived. I well remember going along the back lane to the corner shop in Hyde Park Street with a list of things (bread, small bag of coal) to keep us going until the coal man came. The list would be initialled by my mam, which was a sign that these things would be paid for at the end of the week. Most corner shops operated this system of 'tick' for customers they could trust, but others shops had clocks on their walls that said 'no tick'.

I saw poverty and pride in the bent old lady who lived alone in a room rented from another elderly lady (who needed this little bit of extra money to pay for her own rent.) She was housebound due to her severe asthma and arthritis and needed an oxygen cylinder constantly by her side. Her weekly shopping list included candles (she couldn't afford electricity), bundles of sticks for her fire and a Blue Riband chocolate biscuit for her treat.

There was humour to be found, and people always seemed to find a lot to chat and laugh about in the everyday occurrences around them. Watching a staggering drunk tangle himself up in a skipping rope stretched across the street, and then try to pretend that he wasn't under the influence and his sole intention was to be right there skipping with us kids!

There was also plenty of love and what was missing in life's material possessions was made up for by the abundance of sacrifices made by parents to enable their own children to have a better education; a better start in life for a better future.

I take great pride in the fact that I was brought up in Bensham; within this close working-class community struggling for survival during the post-war years. It has made me fully appreciative of what real life is all about.

I am delighted to have been able to share some of my memories with others within this book. After all we are what our memories have made us, and Bensham has made me the person I am.

Pauline Groundwater
Gateshead, 2003

Pavement group in the open street, 1955. The group includes Elaine Vine, Andrea Mayne, Jacqueline Straughan and Christine Patterson. (Davidson family collection)

Foreword

I was born in the avenues of Bensham in Westbourne, into a typically big family of the day. What do I remember of Bensham? I remember playing football from being very small, and it was often a hell of struggle to get a game. There would be as many as twenty on each side, and the only definite way to get on was if you were lucky enough to own the ball. The lampposts and railings were always in use in the open streets, and if the girls got their ropes up first they would get into trouble with us lot as they were using our goalposts. If it wasn't the streets, then it was the park we were in. I still think about the fun we had around that monkey tree and the sheep dog trials that were once held there.

Other memories? The old railings that were cut down in their thousands when the war effort was on. I think Gateshead must have contributed enough to beat Germany single-handed!

Eric Coates and Brian Murphy and me walking all over – our favourite walk being along the ninepins until we graduated to going along the Fell and ultimately to the Oxford Galleries.

The entertainment was of a simple variety in the close-packed streets. The high point came on Friday nights. It was then the wives could be seen encamped in their doorways 'till late, awaiting their men-folk returning from the pubs to see just how much money remained for the family. I well remember the shenanigans that followed. As more and more skint hubbies stumbled back, the arguments gradually became more public, the theme spread and the subsequent bare-fist fighting was legion. In our street alone there were three big families and we all eventually got dragged into the proceedings. Women would end up fighting women, family got stuck into family and so on, but by the next day we were round borrowing from each other again. Wonderful, I wouldn't have missed it for the world!

Every avenue had its corner shop at the street end. One shop owner at the end of Whitehall Road helped me earn 6d each Saturday by asking me to do things, forbidden to him, on his sabbath. So I went in first thing and opened up the shop, turned the lights on, and was allowed a handful of sweets from a jar before collecting a shiny sixpence left on the counter for me. Nice work!

I had an Aunt Mary who lived in Sydney Grove. We popped into each other's houses all the time, doors were never shut. As I got older and cycled over to St Cuthbert's Grammar, over the water, my journey back from Benwell brought me across Redheugh Bridge and up Derwentwater Road, where, provided my fixed-wheel boneshaker made it, I would stop-off, half way up, at a small shop where the evening papers were dropped off each night. This was where Bobby Gallon ruled supreme. We all worked for him. He always had a cap on, long raincoat, distinctive limp and a woodbine ever-present in Andy Capp style – but he also had a sharp tongue. I have always suspected Bobby Thompson copied Bobby Gallon for his own act!

I would collect my huge bag of newspapers, trying to balance it with my heavy schoolbag on the other shoulder, push my bike up the rest of the bank, ending up walking along Rectory Road delivering papers as I went and going past the mysterious synagogue. I would eventually get to No. 21 Windsor Avenue, where I could drop off my schoolbag and continue down the avenue's four sections delivering as I went; then turn around at Saltwell Park

The Honeysuckle pub on Coatsworth Road, seen in 2002, and quite a bit smarter than in those soot-laden days when Bobby Gallon was an ever-present sight on Sundays, catching the sunshine in his best cap.

delivering all the way up Westbourne Avenue. I'd always have a little chat with Mrs Read in the cobblers shop, as I occasionally struck lucky here and received tickets from her for whatever was showing at the Coatsworth. She got the tickets for displaying bills in her windows.

Each Sunday Bobby Gallon could be found outside the Honeysuckle on Coatsworth Road. The only allowance he'd made for the sabbath was to change his cap!

I will always remember my first infant's schoolteacher at Corpus Christi. She was called Miss Smith. Many years later on *This is Your Life*, Mary Smith was to appear telling tales about me, and stole the show. She was said to have talked endlessly about that night until the day she died – bless her. I was also happy to see many old school mates from Bensham there. Two of them, Billy Currer and Arthur Sober, helped recreate life in the cobbled streets as a short clip for the programme!

When I left school, the authorities hadn't sanctioned Sunday football and so we were careful to adopt a non-de plume. Many was the time that the referee entered names like M. Mouse and D. Duck into his book. I can tell you these names were a good topic of conversation afterwards when we all congregated back with the Jolly Boys in Saltwell Social Club!

I still have family living in this area, and upon each return the trips back become more and more nostalgic as I get older. When I come up I drive around the streets and I remember with fond memories the incidents and the characters. I always like to see my old school Corpus Christi again, as I do John Gibson. We go back a long way, John and I – I first recall him as a young club reporter hovering around us players at Redheugh Park for the crumbs of a story. He was there when I became coach of Gateshead and again during my spell as manager of Sunderland. We've stayed great pals.

A tale from one my return trips, this time in 1981: Here I am, sat outside Mrs Read's old cobbler shop in my big car, wondering who lived there now, when to my surprise she appears at the door. I get out and re-introduce myself. She immediately fetches her husband out exclaiming 'Look who's here, it's the paper-lad!' Now I had just been on every television in

Lawrie McMenemy in the 1970s.

Europe after signing Kevin Keegan for Southampton – and she had called me the paper lad.

Next, she invites me in for a cup of tea, we chat, and shortly before I leave she utters the now-immortal words 'Have you got a job yet son?' I didn't have the nerve to tell her, but, as I left, asked her if she would do me the great honour of switching her television on the next Tuesday night when I was appearing on a chat show. To this day I'm sure that when she saw me that evening, she would have said to her husband 'Eee hin, there's our paper lad again!'

The people of Bensham still don't realise how well-known their area is around the world. My job has taken me on travels all over, and apart from twenty months as manager of Sunderland AFC, we haven't lived in this area now since 1966. I meet entrepreneurs, many performers and some very influential Jewish people and they all talk kindly of Bensham.

It is no surprise to me just how many entertainers know and speak fondly of their Friday evenings in the North East and their time on the Fell.

Now having the luxury of four wheels instead of the two fixed ones on my old bike, I can cover the miles around the area much quicker.

Recently I noticed the tailors shop on Old Durham Road still had the name Renwick Bros now fading on the board. I popped in to ask what happened to the brothers and found they were still sewing away upstairs and making the best made-to-measure suits in the business. Chris, my son, had to endure listening to us three old fellas recollecting those rare old times for ages. The Park and Saltwell Social Club figured heavily.

The tramlines are now no more, gone also are the cobbles and the *Chronicle* doesn't sell a fraction of the load I once carried around these streets, but the memory lingers on, and will continue to do so for some time now, thanks to Pauline's book and others like it. These tales are the fanfare to the common man.

Lawrie McMenemy

1 The Open Street

…The open street – that mighty place of education, the favourite school of Dickens and of Balzac. Suffice to say this; if a lad does not learn in the streets, it is because he has no faculty of learning. It is all around about you and, for the trouble of looking, that you will acquire the warm and palpating facts of life…

(Acknowledgements to R.L. Stevenson)

Loose biscuits

I lived in the Saltwell Road area from 1961 to 1989 before moving to Brighton Road. My husband was born in First Street in 1937, and moved to Trevethick Street as a young lad where he lived most of his life. Bill went to Brighton Avenue school and I think I'm right in saying that his headmaster was a Mr Botcherby. When we lived in Trevethick Street I used to shop on Saltwell Road where we had such a good selection of shops there of all kinds – Carrick's the bakers, Candlish and Beverages and also Charlie Young's, who were butchers. There was also a lovely little grocer's shop called Elsie Lambert's where you could buy butter by the quarter-pound.

At the bottom of Dunsmuir Grove there was a shop called Betty Purvis that sold the most beautiful cooked ham. You could buy loose biscuits from the tins at the Home Bakery.

Mrs Ada W.

Snow

Making a snowman was a joy, and the bigger the better! Sliding was even better and we had a field at the bottom of Angus Road where we spent ages going up and sliding down. As the light faded you could catch us striving to make the slidey even longer and glassier as it began to refreeze. We had to be dragged in with blue extremities and cried as we began to thaw out, dying for a wee.

Next day you could bet some spoilsport had been out covering bits with ashes.

Maria Thompson

Horses

There were still a lot of street horses in use in the late 1940s. The ice cream man, sometimes the coal man, but one of the best was the rag and bone man because we always got a balloon if we could give him some old clothes or scrap. My favourite was the pony and trap. It was a 1d a ride. The carriage was almost round, like a tub, and there was a seat all around the inside ledge. Every May Day all the horses would be decorated.

Maria Thompson

Underneath the arches

I liked the trains, but what I didn't like to do was walk under the arches from Armstrong Street when a train was thundering over it. The arches were usually dirty with lots of green slime covering the walls. I enjoyed lying in bed on a warm summer night with my windows open listening to the goods trains shunting down in Low Fell sidings.

Maria Thompson

Front room shops

There was a little sweet shop near the bottom of Askew Road, a favourite haunt of mine in fact. The lady who worked there was called Charlotte. Many a time I would go in for two ounces of sherbet lemons or chocolate éclairs, my favourites.

A few enterprising old ladies would have their front rooms converted into little shops. One was in Morrison Street, where I lived, and I was often sent there for me mam or Auntie Gina. Auntie Gina wasn't a real auntie, she was me mam's friend. All mam's friends were aunties and uncles then. Mam used to send me with a jug to buy vinegar, and Auntie Gina would send me for bread. This was lovely crusty uncut and by the time I got back with it, all the corners were nibbled off. 'Must have been the mice' she would joke.

Auntie Gina's mother, Mrs Hornsby, Grandma Hornsby to me, had a front room shop in Prest Street. My mother did a lot of shopping there. Eventually Grandma Hornsby's sight started to fail and kids used to go into her

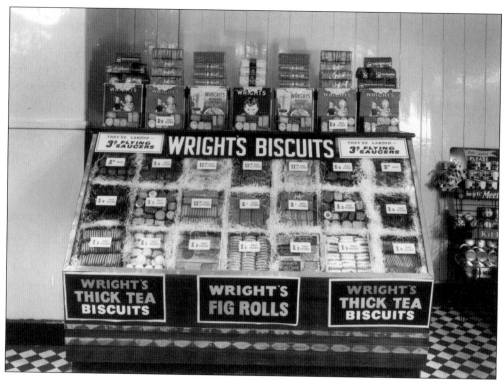

The rosy-cheeked boy on the tin was a source of fascination... (courtesy: Donald Riddell)

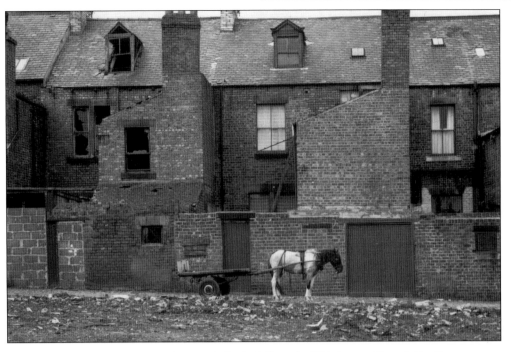

The ragman's horse waits patiently at the top end of Whitehall Road, 1976. (courtesy Trevor J. Ermel)

shop giving her pennies covered in silver paper, getting more than they were entitled. She must have been in her eighties before she had to give up the shop.

Although some women didn't have shops in their rooms they would capitalise sometimes by putting a little table at their front doors and sell toffee cakes and toffee apples that they had just made. Convenient that they were on the route home from school!

Maria Thompson

First launderette

The first launderette that I ever saw opened its doors on Askew Road, and I marvelled at these huge washing machines that just turned the clothes round and round. It seemed an effortless way of doing the washing, but my mam insisted that they couldn't get the clothes properly clean so she wouldn't use them. She kept on with her

old poss tub and wringer. They were all she ever used, even up to 1964 when she died. It hadn't been too long before that that she had been using two flat irons that she heated up on the gas ring on the cooker.

Maria Thompson

Better bets

My dad had a bet on the horses every day. He used the pseudonym XP on his bets (to protect the innocent!). He used these letters because he'd seen big brass ones suspended above the altar in St Philip's church at Dunston. I think he thought they might bring him some blessed-religious luck in his gambling; they never did though, serve him right I thought.

I remember this time we were on holiday and Uncle Geordie was with us. There was a big race on while we were away, so somehow I found a sixpence and put it on a horse. It didn't win and

The launderette or 'Bendix', 1955. (courtesy: Donald Riddell)

as I was a little girl I thought he would have just given me my money back. He didn't.

Maria Thompson

Smoke

There was a police hut at the end of Leshum (Elysium) Lane, where it met with Bensham Road. The policemen would often come over the road to our paper shop, and me mam knew most of the policemen employed there very well. One in particular joined in a plan with me mam to put the frights on me after I showed an interest in wanting to try a cigarette. There was a loud banging on the door of the hut one day and I was asked to answer it unbeknownst. A booming voice said to me 'Is this the place where the little girl smokes woodbines?' I ran off and hid under the table thinking he had come to take me away for being so naughty. I've never smoked since as it happens.

Lena Ireland

Tizer time

Ernie and Hilda Waugh were well known in Bensham. He was the local coalman, and kept his lorry in a garage between Hedley and Trevethick Streets. He was so coal-blackened that few would recognise him off duty. Hilda kept the corner shop on the Stevenson Street end of Newton Street. Us kids could be regularly found there with our pennies and threepences, buying all manner of sweets, now sadly long gone. Some included whirligigs, toffee cakes, parma violets and liquorice root. I would be sent each Sunday for a bottle of Tizer, two silver sachets of Nescafé, and a quarter of Raspberry Ruffles. This would allow us all a teatime treat and get us in good humour before the zinc bath routine began, heralding the end of the weekend.

Susan Bulmer

Full frontal

When I was a lad living in Stephenson Street I went shopping for a Jewish lady called Mrs Sucher who lived opposite us. I remember taking in her shopping one day after her husband had died, and the coffin was standing upright with him on full view at the top of the stairs!

Robert Davidson

Our group sadness

Our group of girls went to the 'inters' club at the church hall. This was for ten-fourteen year olds who were too young for the regular youth club, which you could join at fourteen. We used to walk along the walls on our way, knocking at doors, running, then rushing into a shop on Rawling Road where we'd buy a miners mint which lasted for ages – and all for a penny! It was a huge white mint which gave our parents nightmares if we were caught with them in our mouths, as they repeatedly warned us we would choke, though none of us ever did. It was a strange little shop called Ellams, because half of it was a privately-run library, and the other half a sweet shop. Sadly, one of our group, Linda Bailey, who was a fantastic runner for Gateshead Harriers, was killed one Christmas by a drunken car driver.

P. Davidson

Plate mince

On Saturday mornings Laws stores on Coatsworth Road used to bake the most delicious plate mince pies and apple pies, so if you went up early you could get them still hot from the oven. If you didn't go early they were sold out.

Mabel Thomas

Lamplighters

The lamplighters used to light the gas lamps with a long stick with a light at the end. Someone else used to come along in the morning to snuff them out again.

Mary Davidson

Play in the park

'The Bensham' was on Bank Street. Our Audrey used to come up there with her dad. There used to be an antique shop at the top. They used to have some grand things. Audrey's grandpa Wallace used to go there regular. I have a photograph in Saltwell Park after school; it shows Audrey's dad in a play there with the school. Barney Close School put on a concert beside the towers once.

Violet Wallace

Ice by horse

When I hear the ice cream chimes around the streets today I think of the time in the thirties when the ice cream seller came around with his horse. One minute his hands were pushing some food down into his horse's mouth and the next he was scraping out some ice cream for you! You just accepted it then.

The milkmen would pour out gills into your jug when you ran out to his horse and cart. People never thought to question the hygiene arrangements then.

Reg Charlton

On tick

The shops in the forties were nearly all tick shops. By tick shops I mean you used to go and get your provisions, but asked the shop owner if he would put it on tick until you had the money by Friday pay day. All railway families were in the same apple cart with this and the shop owners had little choice but join in, or lose out to someone who did. Such was the high number of railwaymen in Bensham.

Reg Charlton

A scene from Merrie England *performed by Gateshead Operatic and Dramatic Society. The production was staged in Saltwell Park, 1953. (courtesy: Gateshead Central Library)*

Gossip and snuff

There wasn't anywhere like Saltwell Road for all the shopping there. You got chatting to everyone down the road and it was a time for catching up on all the gossip. I think I can just about remember most of the shops that used to be there. Everything that you ever wanted was there, and there was always a character to be seen about. Sober's paper shop was on the corner of Westminster Street. It had the most awkward little door, so you always tended to knock into someone standing on the other side when you pushed the door open and entered. It smelt heavily of newspaper-print ink; it was a sort of pungent acidy smell. Sober's also sold snuff by the pen'orth and it was put into a little screw of paper. As a child, I used to think only wicked people bought snuff. Emma Sober was a little woman with strange hair. I never knew whether it was a wig, but it fascinated me. It was jet black with tight curls, and she always had a hair net over it. It just never changed one tiny bit and stayed exactly the same all the years I went in.

P. Davidson

Chocolate heaven

I loved the chocolate shop, which was on the corner of Brunel Street and sold every kind of chocolate you could possibly imagine, and sweets in masses of big jars. There were tins of Roses, which you could buy and have weighed out carefully, and then put into white paper bags. There were sarsaparilla tablets, barley sugars, sour plums, pineapple chunks and pear drops that always caught in your throat and made you cough. 2ozs of heaven for a few pennies. But you had to be careful that the sugar didn't skin your throat if you sucked them too hard. They also sold hot, salted peanuts – delicious!

I'm sure everyone local must remember that chocolate shop. It also sold Wall's ice cream in little blocks, and you were given two wafers, or a cornet, which was oblong in shape at the top so the block would fit in.

P. Davidson

The Hadrian

The Hadrian was where you could buy groceries and freshly-cooked meats. It had pictures of Hadrian's Wall around the walls. This was the only shop in the area that sold jellied veal, and they had slabs of fruitcake which they cut into whatever size piece you wanted. Near this was the Tea Company, which became the Fine Fare shop in later years. It was the first self-service shop around.

P. Davidson

Burnt hair

Catcheside's the hairdressers was small inside and there was only room for a few ladies at a time to have their hair washed over the basin. Then some had perms and their hair would be tongued with these horrible-looking tongues, which were kept hot on a machine. They

Alex and Lena, who ran Turnbull's paper shop at the end of Saltwell Road, and still well remembered as the wooden hut. (courtesy: Susan Bulmer)

The Hadrian stores, 1956. (courtesy: Donald Riddell)

The Christmas party, 1959, and the lovely new yellow dress from Shephards. The model is the author. (Davidson family collection)

would hiss when they were applied to the hair. It was rumoured that Mrs Catcheside had once burnt off someone's hair it was so badly singed!

The shop always had a strong smell of ammonia perm solution. Mrs Catcheside was very popular with the old people, but the young ones liked Phyllis, the young girl who worked there because she was a 'good cutter', as we said then.

P. Davidson

Skipping girls

There were seasons for skipping, and we would go to the greengrocers shop to ask for the old ropes that had been around the boxes of fruit or vegetables that had been brought in. We would get these for nothing. We played right across the full width of the street singing:

All in together girls
Never mind the weather girls
When I count to twenty
The rope should be empty…

We would then rush out of the swinging rope and the last two out would have to take the turn of the two who were turning. It was all great fun and there was always plenty of laughter.

Dorothy Dick

Tops and whips

Then the season for tops and whips came in. It was always a bone of contention then as to who had the best top. We used colour chalks and sometimes pieces of silver paper to stick on the surface of the top to make a pretty pattern when the top spun around. It was great unless of course you got your ankles lashed by accident when keeping the top spinning.

Dorothy Dick

Relievo

We played a game called 'Relievo'. An empty can was turned upside-down in the middle of the road, and several pieces of wood or twigs crossed over the top of the can. The players divided into two teams, and each team stood facing each other across the road. The players took it in turn to bounce a sponge ball across the road, and try to knock the sticks off the can. Whichever side knocked the last stick off would then run away and hide. The other side had to try to find them. The aim was to try and get the sticks back onto the can, when the last stick was in place we all yelled 'RELIEVO!' at the top of our voices. This game was very popular with both boys and girls, but sometimes the neighbours came out and chased us off if they thought we made too much of a racket.

Dorothy Dick

had one that came round – us kids would all sing his song, but change it to 'Do you know the muffin man that lives in Lesham Lane…'

Audrey Routledge

Walking with cattle

Although there were trams running, not many people could afford to use them at a one penny fair. They ran from Saltwell Park to the Central station, but most people walked. I remember walking with my father and sisters near Lobley Hill Road when a bull escaped. The cattle used to be herded over the Redheugh Bridge to Marlborough Crescent, where the market and abattoir was. I remember one day a bull had escaped from the farmer and was running wild. My father pushed us into a field and closed the gate and then managed to catch hold of the bull's rope. He hung on to it, as we watched terrified.

Dorothy Dick

Street vendors

Do you remember Vera from the chapel? Her father was a travelling draper who came from Hawick in Scotland. He would go around the doors. The French onion man was a regular. He came with his bike and if you were at grammar school you would try your French on him.

Polly Donkin's girls would come up from North Shields every Thursday. They would come with their creels and baskets and aprons. One girl would get set up on the pavement and fillet the fish there and then. She had her regulars. She had a board over her basket and a very sharp knife to do the filleting. They would go miles a day selling whatever fish was in season.

Do you remember the muffin man? We

Forgotten

Everyone knew everyone else in the streets, especially the kids, so when it was anyone's party we all would join in. I remember knocking on Geordie Nichol's door to go to his party because they'd forgotten to ask me – and I wasn't going to be left out! That's the way it was.

We used to play knocky-nine door and tie knockers together with string. We had many a clip around the ear-hole!

Robert Davidson

Pen'orth please

The Co-op was on Saltwell Road, and in the war my mam would sell her butter rations to get money. She would also get things from the tick man, who would come around on a Friday. She made bread and teacakes, and leafy (or lardy) cake. We had old horsehair chairs that scratched your skin. We were usually given a penny to buy a pen'orth of bruised fruit from Bushel's, on Saltwell Road, or a pen'orth of greasy chips for our dinner!

Mary Davidson

Shoe punch

We were taken to a place called Gillespie's for free shoes because we qualified as being so poor. They punched three holes into our shoes, so we couldn't pawn them, as they were now spoilt.

Miss Shannon was the school board lady who came around if you missed school. I can remember being sent to Rydolph's bakery on a Saturday morning, to buy a threepenny bag of cakes. One day, it rained so much that the cake bag I was carrying got so wet it disintegrated and all the cakes fell out. I got the blame for the rain, as usual.

Mary Davidson

Canny Scot

The Home Bakery was at the corner of Whitehall Road and Saltwell Road. The owner was a man called John Hudd – a canny Scot – obviously quite a God-fearing man because I remember there were quite a few religious texts on the walls. He was a real master baker and baking began very early in the morning. You could buy freshly-baked loaves and teacakes that were still hot from the oven. I can still remember that lovely hot bakery smell that greeted you inside the shop – which was incidentally almost always full to the door. They also made cakes of all varieties, and tray-loads of bread buns, which were one penny each. If you were lucky, you might get an extra bun put in if you bought a dozen. They also sold biscuits, which were in boxes, and you could get half a pound of mixed ones that were put into white paper bags.

P. Davidson

The wee ginger-haired boy

I remember being fascinated by the picture of a little boy with ginger hair and rosy cheeks, on the box containing ginger snaps. There were piles of white bags on a string hung on the counter, but also big sheets of white tissue-like paper in which they wrapped the bread. You could also buy pasties and pies at dinnertime. On a Saturday afternoon, at about 4 p.m., you could go down and get a bag of mixed cakes for

one shilling, so that nothing was leftover, as Sunday opening was unheard of. I remember a lady called Winnie and another cheerful one called Mrs Walker. They served here regularly for years and years.

P. Davidson

Seating problems

Christmas at the infants school at Brighton Avenue was a very special and magical time. We made paper lanterns, Christmas cards and calendars to bring home for our mam. I loved to wear a party dress, which my gran bought me every year, usually with her Co-op divi or Shephards money. I was taken on the No. 54 bus into Gateshead to do this, squashed onto the side seats as the buses always seemed to me, a child, to be filled with elderly fat ladies, and my gran had well-built proportions!

P. Davidson

Kilties

When we got to the store, if it was Shephards, then I got to have a ride on the three-penny horse, which galloped back and forwards, and then on to chose my dress – usually one with plenty of growing room. Shephards was also the place I got fitted for my Kiltie shoes and summer sandals.

P. Davidson

Wizzy money

My gran would sit down on one of the seats provided for customers. Woe betide any children that tried to sit on them! She would pay with the strange-shaped coins that were Shephards own currency. The coins would be put into a can-like container by the shop assistant, and it would whizz along to the cashiers along pipes. The change would come back the same way almost instantly. If it was the Co-op we were going to, then we would wait upstairs in an office place, where everyone went to collect their divis.

P. Davidson

Cattle train

They used to keep the cattle that arrived by train in the fields adjacent to Low Fell station; there was no team valley factories then (1920). Then, when the time was right, they would lead them up over the station, along Saltwell Road, Rectory Road and Cuthbert Street to the Redheugh Bridge cattle market. This happened every Monday. I was about seven years old and couldn't resist following this procession, only I would go beyond the bounds my mother found safe. I remember on one occasion I had followed them right to the bridge and was just standing there when thwack!, my mother had caught up with me! She had been asking around if anyone had seen a small boy, and a neighbour had said 'Oh yes, there was a small boy with the cattle earlier on.' She said 'that'll be our Kenneth.'

I couldn't resist it, all those drovers with sticks and strange cries, not to forget the manure all over the place behind them, but I paid the price for wandering from home.

Ken Routledge

Divi time

When it was dividend time at the Co-op, we would see the same people every time involved in fiddles to beat the huge queues. There was one woman who would regularly come on crutches and the sea would part for her. She would bring all her neighbours' books. When she was done we would see her walking, nay running, down the steps – she would likely get something from each neighbour for

Kiltie week at Shephards, an advertisement from 1957.

The Flying Scotsman *express thunders along towards Deadman's Arch, Elysium Lane, Bensham, 1935. (courtesy The Armstrong Picture Trust)*

saving them the trouble of a long wait. It got so bad we had to have the police in regularly to help with crowd control.

Another common racket were the fellows that would buy up about £100 worth of woodbines, get all the divi money for them, and then go around the factories selling them to the workers there. They were then 2d a packet.

The divi was 2s 6d in the pound. It was good money then. In the best of times there was also a bonus. Some went on holiday with all this!

Ken Routledge

Easy Street

In the Teams they would let people have clubs on their passbooks. This woman would let them and charge about 1s, we knew her as the ticket-woman. You had to have money to justify a club passbook. They would lend their book to neighbours who didn't have money. They were a little like a Christmas club. Our Ronnie had a Christmas club in the Teams.

Audrey Routledge

Best-ever pies

We lived near the bottom of Saltwell Street. I remember a lady called Mrs McGarry who used to make lovely pies and sell them from her house once or twice a week. We would go round the back and up the stairs in her backyard. She made the best steak and kidney pies I've ever tasted. I'm not sure, but I think her husband was a butcher.

Ruby Borlace

Elliot or Hudson?

There were two fish and chip shops where you could buy a 'paper' of fish. This was either a haddock paper or a cod paper. Elliot's was on Rawling Road and Hudson's was on Saltwell Road. Most people kept to the same one, a lot said Hudson's chips were greasier, but both always had long queues, especially on a Friday. A fish paper was about 2/6d (13 pence) and was always wrapped in newspaper. It was still red-hot when you got it home, your hands sometimes burning with fat that had leaked through.

Maria Thompson

Uncle 'trick-cyclist' Alex

Who can forget the sight of me Uncle Alex Davidson? He was to be found each Sunday outside the Stirling House pub selling newspapers. With only one leg (the other taken off surgically due to childhood polio) he was regularly seen along Saltwell Road, on his bicycle with only one pedal, walking crutch slung across his shoulder and weighed down with an overfull bag of newspapers. How he kept his balance was something we could only ponder, especially after drinking a wee bit of the paper money in the pub before he went home.

Susan Bulmer

Fish and chips

Fish and chips were obviously great favourites for growing boys and we were spoilt for choice in our locality. The fish and chip shop that attracted most people was Hudson's on Saltwell Road as it was the cleanest and brightest in the area. It was also, I believe, the first to install one of those modern-looking stainless steel ranges and offer alternatives to cod and haddock!

Ian Hampton

Lawrie's streets

Other fish shops I recall were McHaffrey's, on Saltwell Road, but they had old dark surroundings. Elliot's on Brighton Road besides St Chads church and Fosters, in the next street, was where Lawrie McMenemy used to get his chips. Apart from two fish shops, Saltwell Road also had Crolla's, the Italian ice cream parlour, Hadrian grocer's, the butchers Charlie Young and Sid Beveridge.

An outing to Redcar Races for the men from Saltwell Social Club. Jack Davidson is second from left (1940s).

St Chads church with no houses now, and a gap that has been put to good use in 2000 with a children's playground. (Davidson family collection)

Of course there were also the Co-op grocers, butchers and fruiterers. Sober's the newsagents, mean old Mrs Turnbull, who had a sweet shop at the top of Maxwell Street, and finally, the Home Bakery which sold hot fresh-bread buns for halfpence each to young boys for consumption whilst waiting in the queue at Bells the barber's, next door.

Ian Hampton

Street games

Outdoor games included 'Hot Rice' played with a bat and ball, 'Cannon', which required a tin can, three small sticks and an old tennis ball. 'Relievo', if I remember, was essentially a run and catch game. 'Knocky-nine-door' is probably known to everybody still, and was good fun. Of course conkers and marbles were always popular. Other outdoor pursuits included apple-collecting, from the orchard beside Low Fell station and bird nesting (I'm afraid). Both these latter activities involved keeping a wary eye out for Sergeant Grey doing his rounds!

Ian Hampton

Buckles food

The war also meant an unfathomable number of those unforgettable cold grey Tyneside dawns and the weekly shopping trips with my mam along Saltwell Road to Sid Beverage, the butcher. Production of a ration book meant a small portion of meat, maybe a link of sausage, the odd single egg, some suet, potted meat and a tin of dried egg, which I loved.

I remember the corner shop at the top of the street, 'Buckles' it was called, with its uncut, chemical-free bread, homemade coconut haystack, and the liquorice root when the sweet ration was exhausted.

Ian Hampton

Sunday food

Sunday dinner (served at lunchtime) was the big meal of the week, with meat, potatoes, greens and Yorkshire pudding. Meat during the rest of the week meant Spam with chips, Spam fritters, corned beef with spuds and carrot cake.

Ian Hampton

Coronation Day

Coronation day in 1953 – it poured all day. Nobody in our street had a television. We went to Hedley Street to celebrate with me cousin Alice and her two children. The whole street celebrated in the Club at the top of their street.

Maria Thompson

Buses and trams

The circular bus route through Bensham was very handy. The No. 53 went along Coatsworth Road past Saltwell Park then down to Saltwell Road. The No. 54 did the circle in the opposite direction. I usually got the no. 54 home, but sometimes I'd get the No. 53 if it came first, and go home the long way round rather than stand for a 54 that might not come.

There was a bus strike in the 1950s and I remember having to walk over to Newcastle. I didn't mind really, it wasn't too far over the old Redheugh Bridge. I still preferred to use the Redheugh Bridge for driving – it's less fraught than other routes.

Maria Thompson

Wooden slats

The trams – I can just remember them! They had wooden slats for seats which dug into my knees because I liked to kneel on the seats to look out of the window. Did I imagine an open-top tram? It's too far back in my memory. I seem to remember travelling on the top of one on the way to Saltwell Park with my dad. I liked going to the park to hear the band, to go on the boats, and to play put. I was always disappointed not to be allowed to go into the maze.

Maria Thompson

Askew shops

I loved Saturday mornings. Doing the shopping along Askew ('Askee' to us) Road. Ted, the butcher, and those lovely girls that worked in the greengrocers who put me wise to the fact that the crinkly stuff on onions wasn't paper!

Maria Thompson

The Co-op

Why did we always call the Co-op 'the store'? Everyone knew that you were going to the Co-op when you said that you were going to the store. It was a fascinating cornucopia – bikes, linoleum, furniture, carpet, runners, nylons and corsets. My particular favourite was going up and down in the lift, so much so that my only ambition was to be a lift attendant. Thankfully, I overcame that in later life!

Maria Thompson

Coatsworth Road shopping haven, when trams rumbled along, c. 1920. (courtesy: Gateshead Central Library)

Shehards of Gateshead

Shephards of Gateshead, (the biggest and the best store) was my favourite shop. The upstairs restaurant was excellent and I still miss it. A super cityscape echoed in the murals. Good food. I felt quite posh up there. Christmas bazaars were very much looked forward to then, although I always hated sitting on Santa's knee. Oh the disappointment when I went to see him for a second time (me being greedy) only to come out with exactly the same present that I got the first time.

The luxurious 'schlop' when the canister containing plastic money, and on rare occasions real money, was sucked up to some office somewhere and change came back via the same route. Better still were the old black balls that skittered on a shaky wire contraption above our heads for the same purpose. These, of course, can now only be seen at Beamish Museum.

Maria Thompson

Me cossie

Going to Shephards meant I was going to get some new clothes – Oh joy! Now shall I have the blue sundress with the white spots, or the green one with the white spots? The green one won. Which bathing costume shall I get? There wasn't much choice really, but any cossie had to be better than the white knitted one I'd had up till then!

Maria Thompson

Pawnshop lamb

We often went into the downstairs café (because it was self-service and therefore cheaper). It had a mural of farm animals around the walls, one of which was a horse. I asked my mother what kind of meat you got from a horse. She said 'corned-bean' and I believed her for years. No wonder they called me 'Pawnshop Lamb' (I was then called Maria Lamb).

Maria Thompson

Conventions

Me Uncle Geordie (but not a real uncle) across the road from us, was an illegal bookie, so we always had to use the back door. Because he lived in a long row of terraced flats it was too far to walk around, so we always just cut through somebody's house calling 'Hello Mary Jane', or 'Hello Aunty Maud', as we

Santa comes to Shephards, 3 December 1971. (courtesy: Gateshead Post)

Maria on holiday wearing her lovely Shephards bather – her pride and joy. She is seen with best friend of the moment, Dorothy Poole. (courtesy: Maria Thompson)

toddled through a neighbours house. Nobody thought this was strange, and everyone kept his or her front doors open. Try that now!

Maria Thompson

Sports – greyhounds

One pleasure was to peep through a hole in the fence at the greyhound stadium, at the bottom of Askew Road. Dad actually took me in once; it was great being able to see the whole track instead of just the bit I saw through my peephole.

Maria Thompson

Elastic snapped

I thoroughly enjoyed my time at St Joan of Arc's school. One of the toilets (outside I may add) had an old disused drinking fountain jutting out of the wall. I once had to spend an entire playtime sitting on this drinking fountain because the elastic in my knickers had snapped and I didn't dare walk around. At lunchtime, I ran home with my hands in my pockets holding them up. I didn't have the sense to take them completely off!

Maria Thompson

Early memory – the Coronation, 1953

June 1953, the Queen's Coronation, I was two years old and I remember being sent up the street to watch the television at a neighbour's house. I had been told to go up to Mrs Coe's house to see the Queen. I can remember tapping shyly on the door and somehow thinking that she was the Queen, because I didn't quite understand the concept of television at two years of age, but it seemed crucial to my parents that I did not miss out on this unique occasion!

P. Davidson

The street that disappeared

We lived first in Westminster Street, which consisted of upstairs and downstairs flats with a backyard and outside toilet – no bathroom, no hot water. Bath night was usually on a Friday when the old zinc bath brought in and filled in front of a coal fire. The houses were built on old mine workings with streams underneath, and water suddenly started to appear in the passageways in the houses. When the workmen started pulling up the floorboards to remove the problem all the money I was depositing down the 'moneybox' gaps were discovered and handed back to my parents. These houses were also subject to subsidence. One night a whole row in Westminster Street collapsed right opposite St Chad's church and the people were evacuated into the church hall. The houses were eventually pulled down leaving rather a sinister gap, which is still there but is now used as a children playground.

P. Davidson

Curly cabbages

The street was cobbled and great for street games. The children and adults would congregate during the early evening in the mellowing sunlight. Often a huge skipping rope would stretch across the width of the street with everyone joining in at various opportunities. Other games we played were 'curly cabbages', 'hopscotch', 'What time is it Mr Wolf?' and 'Chasy'.

P. Davidson

Dolly cats

Other games were played with dolls and prams. This often involved capturing a loose cat and forcing it into dolly clothing. They would put up with it so much whilst there was a hint of sweets about, but would eventually dart down the lane with a posse of little girls in pursuit to reclaim the jettisoned clothing before it was lost in some locked backyard.

P. Davidson s

Mud pies

One of the ever-popular street games was making mud pies with the contents of the

Westminster Street showing the row of flats opposite the church before they subsided and were eventually razed completely, c. 1955. The three children are the author (in the kilt), with Elaine Vine and Andrea Mayne. (Davidson family collection)

cracks between the pavements – nothing was wasted in those days! We would dig the muddy filing out with a lollipop stick and keep adding the contents to a dolly's bowl to make a delicious pie. There was always someone dressing up and clanking around in their mother's old high heel shoes or pretend weddings with net curtains for veils. When playing fish and chips shops you could wrap stones and grass up in newspaper, which we imagined smelled just like the real fish 'paper'.

P. Davidson

Night comforts

If you fancied camping you could borrow the old cloth-horse and put a blanket over it. We would picnic with bread and jam and bottles of water in toy tea sets. Then when it was time to go in when the old gas street lamps hissed you could always run and hide behind them until the door was closed. Somehow you then desperately wanted to be on the other side of that door where it was warm and comfortable.

P. Davidson

'Sticks a diddy-o'

We used to have some strange and colourful characters going up and down the street. There was an old lady who was little and bent who sold bundles of sticks. She used to look rather stick-like herself. She wore a cap and smoked a pipe. Her cry would be 'Sticks-a-diddy'.

Another familiar visitor was the rag and bone man with his horse and cart full of all sorts. If you had any rags you might get a few coppers and a balloon. There was another caller who came around shouting 'Any old rags or loom-bar' (lumber). I always wondered what loom-bar was and whether we had any in the house anywhere. Another cry was 'Calla heron' from a man selling fish and herrings. Door to door salesmen were common. My favourite was the 'better ware' man who always gave out tiny tins of polish as samples. I would be given these to play 'house' with.

P. Davidson

2 Home

Hissing gas lamps, warm and mellow
Flickering coal fires, red and yellow
Rocking chair beside the fender
Mother's touch so soft and tender
Family warmth and proggie mats
County caps and best church hats
Grandfather clock ticking slowly
Sundays kept devout and holy
Mother packing father's bait
Home-made bread on willow plate
Co-op butter churns, fresh ground coffee
Apples covered with sticky toffee
Dust-dark miners chiselling coal
Others despairing on the dole
Nostalgic days of happy and sad
When I was just a little lad.
P.G.

Mangle

This mangle was a source of curiosity and allure for me when I was young, and I was always being told 'don't touch that mangle', but I couldn't resist touching those fascinating and tempting cogs, and of course eventually cut my finger in it. I didn't dare tell because I knew I'd be told off with 'I told you so's', so I ran over the road to my auntie (a neighbour friend actually) and she put a plaster on and agreed that this was our little secret. I always remember that she said 'we'll tell your mammy that the cat scratched it.'

Maria Thompson

Saturday teatime

Three things stand out in my memory about Saturday teatime – the smell, the taste and the silence. Mam would be cooking the Sunday joint; usually beef, and the smell would permeate the whole house. I would have bread dipped in the juice and it was heavenly. The silence was always preceded by that signature tune of the football results. Me dad sent in his pools to Littlewoods every week for as long as I can remember and he never won a thing. 'Give the envelope a kiss before you put it in the box' he always said. It must have been the kiss of death, and death is what would have happened if anyone had dared to speak when those results were being read out.

Maria Thompson

Veronica Lamb outside the back door of Morrison Street, c.1935. It gives a tantalising glimpse of the evil finger-jamming mangle, seen darkly within the scullery behind. (courtesy: Maria Thompson)

Winter

We didn't have anything like central heating in those days, only a coal fire. It was so cold in the bathroom at No. 12 Angus Road that the bottle of Iglodine that was kept on the bathroom window froze solid.

When we lived at No. 84 Morrison Street I was very small and sometimes slept on a shakedown in front of the fire with me mam in the kitchen (nowadays called the lounge). What we call the kitchen today was what we called the scullery. When me dad, a pitman, was on night-shift, she used to haul the mattress off the bed and we'd sleep there in front of the fire to keep warm. It was a great adventure for me. We didn't have fireguards either. I also remember her gathering the kitchen fire onto a shovel and carefully carrying it into the bedroom.

Maria Thompson

Wash day

Me mam took in clothes to wash for me Aunty Gina. When it came to the drying, there were no tumble driers and it all had to be hung out, provided it was dry. If it was wet out it was miserable inside the house. Ironing was fun. She had two flat irons that were heated on the gas ring. She didn't exactly spit on the irons to test them but wet her finger and would quickly touch one to see if they were hot enough, this had them spitting back in reply. When ironed, they were hung up next to the roof on a line that criss-crossed the ceiling. A bird got in one day and got tangled in the washing, messing it. She wasn't pleased to have to do them again.

Maria Thompson

The washing at the mercy of coal smuts from passing trains (courtesy: Ken Groundwater)

It shook the house

I used to go to a youth group at a church on Rawling Road but beyond going to a cinema there wasn't a lot to do outside the house in my day. My step dad Alec lived in a little flat on the site of the workhouse, near Fountain View. Before that we all lived in Watt Street, right down at the bottom end near the batteries and the main railway line. Passing heavy trains made the house shake. I recall we must have been close to a point where they occasionally had to stand because once the steam engines set off again my mother's washing captured a fair few smuts as they gently fluttered down to our level below.

Lena Ireland

Bonnie baby

My mother Jean Beattie won first prize once in the teams charity baby show. She was dressed in a hand-knitted suit, which was made by her own mother, my grand-ma, Dolly. With the prize money, Dolly had Jean's photo taken professionally.

Ann Jones

Dolly

My grandmother Dolly Robertson used to wash every Monday morning, as this was traditionally washing day in the Bensham area. Dolly started early possing the clothes and would only break off to buy the fresh or calla herring from the fish man or woman doing the back lane rounds with their horse and cart, or even barrow. While she was drying the clothes Dolly baked bread and rolls to eat with the herring. It's a scene I remember clearly in the house when I was a child; a tea towel over the rising dough in front of the coal fire and the smell of cooking bread and damp clothes every Monday.

Ann Jones

Bonnie baby Jean Beattie, 1929. (courtesy: Beattie Family)

Steamy depths

The mangle stood in the scullery on a dull silver-metal stand, the two sides forming matching triangles with four bars along the floor forming a rectangle for stability. Two cream-coloured rollers were turned, with much huffing and puffing, by a handle on the right-hand side. There were murderous exposed cogs at the side of the rollers, just big enough to trap this toddler's fingers in... it wasn't called the mangle for nothing!

There was also the boiler, a big metal thing on legs, with a lid on the top. Clothes disappeared into its steamy depths along with the dolly blue, which did look like a little doll. The frightening process of dropping clothes into the red-hot water, while trying not to splash, was matched only by the even more

Dolly Robertson from Hedley Street on washing day – and ready for anything, c.1930. (courtesy: Beattie family

and eventually got rid of him. About a year after, I starting going out with Audrey's dad, who I had previously known at school. I didn't think much of him then. He lived opposite the school for a time and his own father was in the army at the time. When we were coming out of school, he and his brother Arthur used to wait for us at a corner with sticks and things and they terrified me. I got granny out to deal with them.

Violet Wallace

Mary Jane Donnelly in 1920, grandmother of Mary Davidson. (Davidson family collection)

frightening procedure of getting the clothes back out again. My mam used a special stick for this – but not the wimpish tongs used by other mothers – and I realised to my horror just how easy it was for the clothes to slide back under. I never mastered the technique like me mam did. The boiler was also handy for drowning unwanted kittens in, and so unfortunately, in my child's mind, it became associated with death.

Maria Thompson

Courting

I was married in 1934 but it wasn't to Leslie Cole. He used to come to Shephards every Saturday evening with big bunches of flowers. All the men did at that time. He was a cricketer and he used to keep going away playing for Gateshead Fell. I didn't want that

Wages

When I was first married my husband got £14 a month, which was a lot in those days. We paid 17/6d a week rent, which was a lot, and he got 5 shillings a week pocket money. He would hand over his pay and I gave him his pocket money. Audrey was born in Silverdale Terrace.

Violet Wallace

Puddings

My Mam had an old pot boiler which she used to put the Christmas plum puddings in to boil. We called them pot-puddings.

She had velvet across in front of the fireplace as an ornament. She had an old hearth, with a boiler on one side and the oven on the other. The oven was called the range. At the weekend we all got bathed in the tin bath in front of this fire. I got in first. My mother used to boil beetroot every Friday night – it was lovely. Home-baked bread as well. We had good solid food when we were young, there was none of this going out for rubbish then (1915). If we had money on the Friday night we might sometimes get some chips to go with our meal. We never got fish. We used to get our tops and whips from Donaldson's, and colour the tops in. The shop is still there but under a new name. Mark Tony's ice cream used to come around in a barrow pushed by a man. It was lovely.

Violet Wallace

Milko

The milkman's horse knew where to stop for deliveries. The milk was in big churns. Our milkman was called Thompson. When we were sledging we knocked the churn over – we all had to club together to pay for it – it

was a full churn! Those were the days! Every so often we used to get a ride on his horse and cart up and down the street, which was a real treat for us. The ice cream man used to come to Whitehall Road School with ice cream in a barrel. It was 1s 2d for a cornet.

Violet Wallace

Keystones (1914)

There used to be policemen knocking about when I was little and we were terrified of them. If you were seen kicking a ball about or playing a game called 'bays' we were chased by these policemen. We used to get chalk and chalk-out all these bays on the pavement that's how we used to make our entertainment then.

Violet Wallace

Clarkie's

My father was a draughtsman and worked at Cowens Sheldon at Carlisle at first. My mother was a tailoress and could make all our clothes and did. He eventually got a job a Clarkie's in Gateshead (Clarke Chapman's Heavy Engineering) he worked there for well over forty years. I have a picture of me father, Robert Holmes; he's sat at the drawing board at Clarke Chapman's. He trained dozens of apprentices. He was smart and always wore a bowler hat. Audrey's dad was discharged from the Second World War due to a bad chest; the doctor said he should never have been admitted in the first place.

Violet Wallace

Daughters of Temperance

We moved into a storehouse that once belonged to the Co-op in Camborne Grove. We were lucky to have a good landlord in Jack

The dapper Robert Holmes, at his draughtsman's desk at Clarke Chapman's, c.1920. (courtesy: Audrey Stephenson)

Smith. If you wanted anything doing he would do it. I was married from there. I was in the Recobites when I was little, it was in a place opposite the Mulgrave baths – the 'Daughters of Temperance' the hall was called. Eleanor Swinburne and me used to go.

Where Durham Road church is was once Abbots school for naughty boys. Higher up was a fountain and that's why this street is called Fountain View.

Violet Wallace

Delicate flower

I was little when the First World War was going on. My sister was nearly six years older than me and she had to look after me, as I was delicate when I was a child. Look at me now,

ninety-three and still going strong! She died when she was eighty-two. My Mother would say to her 'Look after our Violet.'

Violet Wallace

Work rest and (no) play

Gateshead enginemen got the reputation for being in only three places throughout their working lives. They were either in their beds, the pub or at work. There was no time for anything else in their lives. If you accepted this was your lot you eventually made a good railwayman. You couldn't go out for a drink before your turn of duty, but by heck they got their own back on the licensee when they came off duty. It was a difficult thirst to slake after you had shovelled seven or eight tons of coal for five hours solid.

The women folk married to railwaymen always knew where their men were. They were in the house sleeping, or the other two places, pub or work. This encouraged very steady relationships believe it or not. There were very few divorces then 'cause firstly the men had little opportunity, or energy left, to stray, and secondly it was difficult to be romantic in greasy, oily overalls!

Reg Charlton

Blue bags

My granny used to take in other peoples washing to get a bit of extra money. I remember the big pulleys from one end of the room to the other, and the blue bags that she used in the wash. She also had a row of flat irons along the fireplace that were big and black. She was funny and had some saying that amused us kids. One was 'one day aal wake up and find mesel deed…'

Mary Davidson

…It was so cold the Iglodine in the bathroom froze…' (courtesy: Donald Riddell)

Wash day Windsor

Washing day was always on a Monday, in fact it began on a Sunday evening with the hustle and bustle of sorting and getting things ready for the 6 o'clock start next day. The pot boiler (made with bricks) was in the scullery and the fire was lit underneath to heat up the water. This was poured into the posse tub and my mam used a wooden dolly. Later on, when things modernised, she used a vacuum posser. My mother was very fussy about her washing. Everything was scrubbed with a block of Windsor soap and scrubbing brush, then rinsed and scrubbed again. Whites were put into a bowl of starch. We had a great big mangle to wring things out, then they were put out on a pulley in the yard or back lane. If any horses and carts came along then the washing was rushed in. When it was dry, it was all ironed with flat irons, usually two, so that one was heating on the fire while the other was being used.

Dorothy Dick

Pauline and Gran, c. 1953. (Davidson family collection)

Dorothy Dick (against the window) with a group of friends on a church outing.

Superstition

Me mam would fall for the gypsies every time, she was terrible, she was so superstitious. When people were out of work, me mam always helped by buying something small off them cause she knew they were on hard times. One sold blue mottled soap that nearly took your skin off! Another sold tea.

When we were kids and if we saw a magpie, we would always say to it 'Good morning Mr Magpie, how's your wife and family?' A lot of people were very superstitious, especially about magpies. Farmers didn't like the magpies.

Audrey Routledge

Home fires

I lived in Stephenson Street, which was a street off Saltwell Road. It was a rented flat with three bedrooms. There was no hot water, no electricity. It had gas mantles, a coal fire with a big black range oven, which my mother used for baking and cooking. We would burn almost anything to keep the fire going. This included any old shoes we found, and firewood from the sticks man. I remember it was a penny for a bundle of wood. Waugh's coal business was at the top of the street. I used to do some shopping for Mrs Waugh and for this I got a scone. I went to the store (Co-op) for her, to buy oats for the horse. The stable was next to a big house at the top of the street. The coal was delivered to them and the Waugh girl's, Annie and Ada, used to bag it. Hilda Waugh ran a shop in Newton Street and Jackie and Ritchie Waugh went round with the coal on the horse and cart.

Robert Davidson

Jugs out

Elsie Lambert used to push a barrow around with a big milk churn on it, and people used to rush to get their jugs out and get them filled up.

Robert Davidson

Stick man

I used to take my father's only suit to the pawnshop each week, for my mother, and get it back before the weekend, so that he never knew. My mother baked all her own bread in the old black range and did her best for us, but she had a hard man in my father, and deserved better. He had two sides. There was one for the family, and one for the outside world.

He was nevertheless a good first-aider in the St John's. He kept an allotment down Teams area and worked at the coke ovens near Lobley Hill. I used to go around with the stick man sometimes and he would give me a penny for helping. I could then go to the matinee on the Saturday at the 'Pal'.

Me clothes were cut-downs so that the trousers would be baggy like old men's, and my jumpers were raggy. The teacher once gave me a pair of boots; they were my pride and joy.

Robert Davidson

The Teams

I was born 1928 at No.47 Vine Street in the Teams area. I can't remember much about the house, but I remember cockroaches and other bugs used to climb up the walls. There was Vine Street Mission nearby with St Winifred, who everyone knew as she ran the mission. There was an ice-cream barrow with Manzies ice cream, Murphy's coal business, and a fruiterer on Askew Road. My granny used to

clean for someone called Hughes. There was a pawnshop called Davison's on the same block. I think the nearby chemist shop was called Gayle's. We stayed in my granny's front room at this time, but moved to Queen Street, which was close to Victoria Road, a little later. I think I remember my father pushing a barrow full of our things when we made this change. Then, from the Teams area, we moved up to Bensham, into an upstairs flat in Armstrong Street, off Saltwell Road. We made another move after a little time to Hyde Park Street, and then to Saltwell Street.

Mary Davidson

Handlebars

The means test person used to come. My father didn't work. We slept four to a bed and put coats over the bed in winter. We never had pyjamas, but slept in what we called shifts. That's all we had – there were no sheets or pillowcases on the bed.

In Saltwell Street, next door to us, the lady there took snuff and used to buy a pen'orth from the newsagent. I remember her son used to work at the Co-op delivering milk. He used to bring his horse into the backyard and they also had chickens running up and down the back stairs. Eileen Hardman lived next to us on the other side and used to take her father's suit to the pawnshop on Redheugh Road, putting it over the handlebars of her old iron bike.

Mary Davidson

Purple haze

Granny's dinners were the meat, gravy and mashed potato type meals – she had a 'tatty beater' which she used with great vigour, for her mashed pots and turnips and threats! Puddings were mostly rice, or barley and

Mary Davidson with brother-in-law Harry and sister-in-law Stella, enjoying a nostalgic moment amid a recreated miner's cottage at Beamish Open Air Museum, 1986. (Davidson family collection)

raison, and home-made soup was made with ham-bone stock and filled with lentils, leeks, carrots, turnips and sometimes potatoes.

My gran also made fruit pies; she loved to get bilberries when she could, and I loved to put milk over and make everything go purple, my tongue into the bargain. Gran was a widow, so she had a tough job as she also had polio that left her with one leg shorter than the other. She was also rather large and raised her family with many a crack over the head. She was never anything but kind and very generous to me, and took an interest in everything I did until she died in 1982 aged seventy-nine.

P. Davidson

Flying shovels

Our landlord had a middle-aged daughter whom everyone called 'daft Doris.' Doris could be perfectly normal one day, and the next day she would be brought back home after roaming around swinging a shovel which she had thought was her handbag, She always wore far too much bright red lipstick, and was rather large in build, so she was quite an alarming sight to a small child.

P. Davidson

First television

I was around nine when we had a television come into the house. Before that, we would all pile into Grant's house at the top of Hedley Street, to watch children's programmes through a magnifying glass attached to a tiny television screen. Watching a black and white test card while waiting in eager anticipation of something coming on was mesmerising.

Susan Bulmer

Bath night routine

The zinc bath was a hoot! This weekly ritual was mostly on Sunday night. The bath was taken down from where it hung in the backyard; it was brushed out to get rid of any spiders or creepy things, then swilled around with some water before being taken indoors to the scullery, as the kitchen was then called. It then took an age to fill using water heated on the gas stove in all manner of pans and kettles. A quick sprinkle of soap powder, (bubble bath was for the rich folk) and we were in, our Judith first, as she was the eldest, then little me, by which time the bubbles where flat, and the water was luke-warm, the remedy for this was of course yet another pan of boiled water. After the bath it was a quick drying down in front of the coal fire, finger and toe nails cut, hair rubbed very hard and then attacked with a wire brush and a fine-toothed comb, to ensure that we did not have or were ever likely to get 'lodgers' as mother used to call them (headlice to you and me).

Susan Bulmer

Old geysers

Two things happened (around the early sixties) which would revolutionise Sunday nights. The first came in the form of the hot water geyser. What joy to simply turn on the tap instead of boiling endless pans! The second was the arrival of the 'coffin' sized bath. Like the little bath it hung outside on the wall and the routine was the same, but it was big enough for Judith and I to get in it together, so finally I got my share of the hot water and bubbles!

Susan Bulmer

If you knew Susie...

The year of the Coronation I was four – too young to fully understand what it was all about, but old enough to know that there was to be a party, and out in the street no less. The newspapers were full of it. Hustle and bustle, Union Jacks and party hats, but boy did the rain put paid to the street idea. However, people, sandwiches and sausage rolls were quickly relocated to the Saltwell Club at the top of Hedley Street. It was there that I would have my 'stage debut'. All of us kids were cajoled, some might even say bullied, into performing a 'tern'. My sister Judith, Dorothy Coates and myself, got up on stage and gave a dreadful rendition of 'If you know Susie'... I've never been so embarrassed or felt so stupid in my life since, and left the stage in tears. However, it was soon forgotten and all had a grand time.

Susan Bulmer

Nine in the beds

There were nine of us at home so the girls shared a bed and the boys another. We had to put coats and anything we could find over the bed to keep warm. My father made proggie (hooky) mats out of rags and hession sacks. He would put a pattern on the hession, and old pieces of cloth or rags were woven into the mats. My father made a new mat every year for Christmas Day.

I remember he also made 'mistletoes' out of the hoops from the butter barrels. He would decorate it with baubles and hang it up for Christmas instead of a tree. He also toasted bread on the fire with a big toasting fork and roast peanuts with salt placed on a shovel and suspended over the fire. We had a big bleezer (draught enhancing shield) that went over the fire to help it get started quicker and make it burn up fast.

Mary Davidson

Robert Davidson's Grandmother and Grandfather Mr and Mrs Fallon. They proudly present three of their four children in this typical 1900 portrait studio view. The little girl is his mother, Anne Isabella, and one of her brothers. The baby is Frances Alice Fallon. (Davidson family collection)

No green

My mam made stottie cakes every week, but one thing she didn't like was anything green in the house because this colour was associated with the little people. I believe my great-grandmother Donnelly who spoke in a soft brogue handed this little gift down to us.

Mary Davidson

Behind you…

When we first married we moved into rented rooms in Westminster Street. It was a horrible creepy house with stuffed animals up the dark staircase, and I always felt that there was someone behind me on those stairs. The house seemed full of stuffed birds. It was also overrun with mice that ran up the walls at night, and when you baked you had to cover things up straight away because the mice freely ran across the benches. One mouse even made a nest in my boots.

Mary Davidson

Journey into space

We had good neighbours; there was Mrs Davidson downstairs and the Stuart's, the Martindale's and old Mrs Coe, who had the corner shop. I knew the time by the church clock on St Chad's striking out the hour, and I could see the clock face from the back windows. Times were hard just after the war, and things were hard to come by with rationing going on to 1953. We bought a table and sideboards second-hand and we bought two cups and things bit by bit from Woolworth's. Allan worked long hours and awful shifts doing sometimes sixteen hours away firing on the railway and no one ever knew when their man would return in those days. We would go to the Pal for a treat and listen to the wireless at night, we loved Dick Barton and Journey into Space.

Mary Davidson

Shared the scullery

It only cost £234 17s to furnish our two rooms at No. 23 Hedley Street in 1950. I worked at a shop on Saltwell road to pay the monthly payment of £8 10s while Jimmie walked to Watergate pit every day to feed and clothe us. We lived with my mam and dad and brother. We had the front room and shared the scullery. The toilet was in the backyard and the long tin bath that hung on a hook in the yard was the bath. The three bedrooms upstairs were split between the family.

Jean Beattie

Cald'warmed

A weekly outing for me was to go to the allotments near the racecourse estate every Sunday morning for the fresh mint for the Sunday roast. On the way back I used to call at Hilda's shop in Newton Street and pick up the Nuttalls Mintoes. After dinner the sweets were laid on the hearth to soften ready to eat in the afternoon after Sunday school, where I was a teacher. Another Sunday tradition was to keep some meat, potatoes and vegetables back from the dinner to fry up on Sunday night. This was called 'cald'warmed up' to us.

Sunday was also a day for calling on my friend, Linda Bailey, to go to Saltwell Park which was our favourite haunt. We used to play tennis, go in the rowing boats and, in earlier years, catch tadpoles in the lake. Sometimes we would just lie in the sun and listen to the band playing.

Anne Jones

Moving on

I was born on 5 July 1921 in Orton Street and we moved into Second Street after a short time. My father James had come over from Northern Ireland for work. We had no radios or television was a thing of the distant future. Life was all cards or playing in the street then. At home was my brother James and sisters Winifred and Thelma. Thelma was a bit accident-prone – she was the one we had to fish out of the lake in Saltwell Park.

I met my husband, Ted Ermel, at the place most romances began in those days; the Oxford Galleries dances in Newcastle; something of a cattle-market at times, but it was certainly the place to find romance.

We got married on 19 October 1949 at All Saints church at Lobley Hill, and began our married life in Dean Street, Low Fell, in an upstairs flat. Ted went into the Merchant Navy and happily survived the experience.

Muriel Ermel

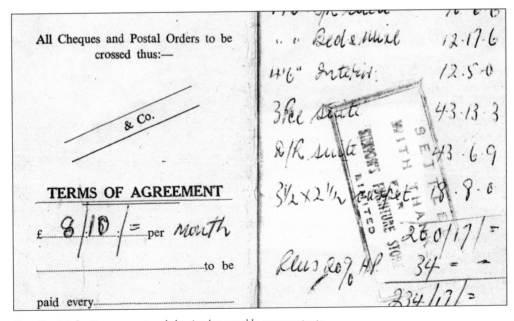

Jean Beattie's furniture payment card showing her monthly repayment rate.

3 High Days and Holidays

The street is as busy as busy can be
For the yearly outing down to the sea
Climb on board and shut the door
Yes, there'll be room for just one more

A great shout goes up as the bus pulls away
At Tynemouth they all mean to spend this
fine day
Ma, where's me bucket? Ma, are we there?
Ma, canna swim if the weather stays fair?

And soon by the sea-front the trip bus arrives
A marvellous day in everyone's lives
They're all there together, both young and old
They might even paddle unless it's too cold

Up go the deckchairs and up goes a tent
Who cares today what money is spent
Here's ya bucket son, divvent be a pest
Today's ya mothers well-earned rest

The children go off in a world of their own
Far from the old house in which they have grown
Potpies and castles are built in the air
And mother at last has some time just to stare

At 12, on the dot, the bait box comes out
There's no time now for the boys to shout
Egg buns and cheese buns and food galore
Better leave room, for there's plenty more

Time for the games now "Geordie de ya best"
His ma says he's always such a pest
Get the ball out, Jinmies in goal
Offside Willie Smith, the ball hit the pole

Now a remembrance of that fine day
Apart from the memories, they'll carry away
So gather yerselves about in a group
There must be a photo of this merry troop

They're all on the bus now, time to go back
Willies on nights and he doesn't want the sack
Back to the cobbles and slate roofs grey
'Yes' they agree 'it had been quite a day'.

P.G.

My grandparents

Both of my mother's parents were dead so I only had one set of grandparents. When I was seven we moved from Morrison Street to Angus Road to be next to them. I remember my grandmother was always knocking on the wall with her walking stick and mam and me would raise our eyes and say, 'What does she want now?'

New Year's Eve was fun though. We always went into their house and they told us the same stories year after year and I laughed at them every year. In fact I would have been disappointed if they hadn't told them.

Granda, being the eldest, was given the honour of being first foot. One year he went out with his lump of coal. Twelve o' clock struck and we waited for his knock on the

High days and holidays.

door. We waited and waited and waited. My dad, who was always ready with a quip, said '...if he doesn't hurry up he'll be carrying a bit of palm when he comes in.'

Granda smoked a pipe. So did grandma. She usually smoked a little white clay pipe. I liked to get it second hand for blowing soap bubbles. 'Don't tell Camille' she would say. Camille was my cousin. What my Grandma didn't know was that Camille already knew she smoked a pipe and many a giggle Camille and me had about it.

Maria Thompson

Christmas

Every year Aunt Gina brought a chicken. In the 1940s this was a luxury believe me! She didn't, as far as I can recall, have to pluck it but me mam did have to clean it out. Many were the bowls of bloodied water I saw at Christmas. We had nuts and tangerines too but always a box of dates was there which I wasn't keen on. The date boxes I liked because of their shape, and tried to transform them into sandals – I should have said only when they were empty!

Maria Thompson

Phew...

Christmas morning was magic. My presents were almost always left on the same armchair, every single time. They were never wrapped the way presents are now but in sorts of rough mixtures.

I used to rush out of the bedroom into the living room to see if 'he' had been. One Christmas morning I was straining to see over the table and when I got a view saw that it was empty. Heck! He hasn't been, but on looking further saw that Santa had left his presents on the settee. Phew, a close thing!

I always had to leave off playing to go to

mass. That's a bit boring when you're only five. Boxing day always seemed to be an anti-climax, until me mam started taking me to the pantomime at the Theatre Royal.

Maria Thompson

Trips

I remember going on a trip with most of the people in Morrison Street. The bus couldn't leave until the pawnshop opened so as one of the mothers could get some money.

Maria Thompson

Space invader

Although their own son had grown up, Uncle Geordie and Auntie Gina still bought stacks of fireworks every year to set off for all the kids in our street. One year I remember my friend Dorothy saying that Uncle Geordie hadn't let go of a rocket in time and it had taken him right over the rooftops and into our back lane. Despite the fact that Uncle Geordie must have weighed fifteen stone, I still believed her...

Maria Thompson

Bonfires

There was always a big bonfire on the pit field, just off Askew Road, and every back lane had its own fire. When I reached my teens I used to go to my school-friend's house in Brussels Street. We'd roast potatoes in the bonfire. Although I loved fireworks, I was terrified of bangers and particularly of jumping jacks. I was such a wimp I wouldn't even hold a sparkler.

Maria Thompson

Pride and joy

There is a picture of myself taken when I was about five years old in the backyard in Hedley Street. The birds in the aviary behind belonged were me dad, Jimmy Beattie's, pride and joy. He spent so many happy hours tending the birds and only gave up the hobby when the corn became too expensive to buy. I am all dressed up and ready for the yearly street trip to Cullercoats, which was organized by Dolly, my grandma. It was always a good day out. The women provided seaside sandwiches and went for the jug of hot water to make the tea when we got there.

Street outing to Tynemouth, 1940s style. The little girl with all the hair (second front row thrd from right) is Mary Davidson, and her grandmother, Peggie, is the lady in the potpie hat.

We played on the penny slot machines and went on the rides in the Spanish city. My granddad, Charlie Robertson, joined the men and went to the bar and, as you can imagine, it was quite a merry trip in the bus on the way back home!

Anne Jones

Fizzy pop

Birthday parties were big occasions and very exciting because of the food and games. You always took a small present and put on your party frock. There was pass the parcel, put the tail on the donkey, musical chairs, the feather bed and postman's knock. Then you had tea, which was a scone with money in the middle wrapped up in greaseproof paper, sausage rolls, sandwiches and birthday cake, which you took home. Everything was home-made and no one would think of buying. There was also jelly, ice cream and fizzy ice cream soda pop, or dandelion and burdock – if you were very lucky. If you didn't have enough chairs to go round the table then you could usually borrow long forms from the church.

Anne Jones next to her father's (Jimmy Beattie) aviary in Hedley Street and all dressed up for the street trip.

A studio group photograph after an outing to Tynemouth in 1938, captured Mary Christie with her daughter Dorothy Peggie, and grandchildren Mary, Rosina and John.

Most parties lasted two hours, and a parent picked you up, but you always hoped to be the last one to go, as you never wanted it to end.

Mrs A.M.

Christmas every week

They get far too much now, the bairns. We were looking forward to Christmas for months before – now it's Christmas every week. We always got at least an apple and an orange. At Easter we would go around our friends and give them a dyed egg in exchange for one of theirs.

Violet Wallace

Christmas and carols

Christmas was a wonderful time for us children, as we all firmly believed in Santa. In

47

Church forms were frequently borrowed for parties. Included in posing in this back lane party picture are Margaret Woodhall, Andrea Mayne, and Maureen Duffy, three children from Westminster and Saltwell Street.

fact we did until we were about eight or nine years of age, and after that the doubts crept in. We didn't have a long list of things we wanted, like now, just one main item for Santa to bring. We had to hang our stockings up on the fireplace on Christmas Eve. We were thrilled with simple things like a packet of sweets, an apple or orange, and sometimes a three-penny or even a sixpence piece that we would find the next morning.

My father would make the most wonderful small toys for us. He made shops and all the little containers with sweets to put into the shop. The Sunday-school party was the highlight, when Santa arrived just before we left, and we all got a very little present. We thought this was great. Another thing we could do was go out early on Christmas Eve and sing carols. I loved every bit of this.

Dorothy Dick

Joy has come

After choosing the party dress, it was carefully hung up until the party. We had to pay one shilling for our own food, which was a paper

Weddings 1920s style! A High Day for Dorothy Christie (with beret) at a cousin's wedding.

bag with a pasty or meat square, coconut snowball and another cake. Milk was kept for the afternoon so you drink it with the food at your desk in the classrooms. After this there were party games in the hall.

Then the exciting bit – the Christmas tree, which had been concealed behind a big screen. The headmistress would move the screen as we all sat on the floor and sang:

Light the candles, deck the trees
Joy has come to you and me
Joy, joy at Christmas-time
Joy at Christmas-time…

The candles – real ones – were then lit and this was the magic of Christmas.

P. Davidson

A visit to the face

There were pits all over the Gateshead area and were still working in the 1920s. There was the Betty and Ann pits, the Ann had a pond. There was the Park drift next to the Coach Road. They were all linked underground with the Glamis pit and into the Jarrow and Pontop wagon-way that ran down to Jarrow Staiths. The family knew this deputy and one day I said to him I would love to come down. He said 'right-o' and I said 'can I bring me two mates?', he said 'OK'. So we went down the Shop pit this Sunday. We got kitted out with lamps and matches. The first thing that hit me was the surprise of seeing all the horses, all kept at the bottom of the shaft, where it was all white-washed. It was beautiful.

The guide – a young lad – said 'The fellow you want is along there' and he led the way. He led on and on and I noticed that the shaft size was getting smaller and smaller. We were passed by a group of miners coming back off the face and struggled to pass them. The guide said they had come off a conveyor belt that led right under

Sunday best! Mary Peggie, sister Rosina and friend Eileen Hardman in 1940. Mary and Rosina's father had the dresses made up in Birmingham where he was temporarily working. They were blue, and the girls' pride and joy, but note the sandshoes – they had no party shoes!

Ravenswood Castle. We noticed the speed these fellows came through. They expertly sped along even though their heads were maybes an inch from the top of the passage, so adept were they at moving about with their backs permanently bent. 'They are making for the pithead baths' he said.

The height was now 3 feet and the lad said 'I know, I'll take you through a short-cut.'

This short-cut turned out to be no more than 18 inches high and our backsides were bouncing off the roof as we were hurried along. Eventually the guide says 'They are in there.' We peered through this hole – just big enough to crawl in and there was the man I knew working this huge coal-cutting machine with two others. 'What took you?' were his first words.

These fellows knew nothing else than this

Tommy Lamb showing visitors a new piece of machinery down the pit.

work, and probably their father's as well! I would have hated it down there. It was an experience, but I was pleased to get out I'll tell you. There was a pitman's bus used to run from Kibblesworth to the top of Chow-Dean bank every day.

Ken Routledge

The bus trip

Street trips to the coast were the great outings of the summer. Doors were knocked on, numbers taken, and money paid every week towards the cost.

Activity flourished; eggs were boiled, a mountain of bread was buttered, tomatoes and fruit packed into brown paper bags, custard creams, fairy cakes and, if you were lucky, a few sweets all joined the endless flasks of tea, crockery and cutlery in the shopping bags draped with the picnic rug.

We eagerly awaited the arrival of Thirlwell's coach (the 'trip-bus' to us kids) there were shuffles for the window seats, and 'who would sit in the front, or back' questions being asked. Eventually bags were all packed-in, kids and adults all accounted for, and we were off.

We had fun with the sand and water, ate the lunch with gritty hands, were eventually red raw from being rubbed down with damp towels, and drooled over the ice cream cornet with chocolate flake, such luxury!

Day over, the singsong on the bus home was a little more than us children could bear, and we snuggled down with our mam's. The day ended with the chink of coins as the hat went round to tip the driver.

Susan Bulmer

Thirlwell's Bluebird 'trip-bus' waits patiently in the background for the Hedley Street outing to begin in 1957. From left to right are: Jean Beattie, Sally Birbeck, Alice Cuthbertson (Susan's mam) and Ella Patterson.

Alice Lamb and neighbours from Morrison Street. The neighbours include Elsie Shields, Bella Shields, Ginny and Mrs Phillips.

4 Work

Life was hard throughout the day
And poverty was rife
Hours of toil with little pay
To take home for a wife

Factory grease and factory oil
Work, labour, sweat, toil
Morn 'til noon and noon 'til night
Cranking tools with all our might

The factories took us as a rule
At thirteen, fourteen straight from school
We'd scarcely learnt to count to ten
Before becoming little men

If lucky we were taught a trade
A wage rise if we made the grade
We didn't dare to answer back
Or else we knew we'd get the sack

Now derelict old factories stand
While nature claims her share of land
And bright new units spring up fast
To wipe away the stains of the past.

First encounter

My recollection of Bensham in the winter of 1962/63 was living in digs in Saltwell Road. My employers, the Post Office, had transferred me from County Durham to Newcastle and Gateshead district to work on the counters. My bedroom adjoined the local storeroom and as I worked late shifts, the noise of boxes being moved and banged against the wall very early, too early in fact, became my alarm clock. The culprits remain unknown to me, luckily for them.

I remember travelling to work on chocolate-coloured double-decker buses numbered 53 and 54. The one I got most frequently was the No. 54 over the bridge, I would then change onto a yellow Newcastle Corporation trolley for the last stage of my journey up the West Road.

One of the first unexpected sightings after arriving in this area was seeing the pub near the Co-op called the Stirling House. This was strangely unexpected to me because my hometown was Stirling and I never discovered the connection with Scotland.

Peter McCallum

Working down the pits

My dad was a pitman. In 1947, when I was four years old, he was working at Watergate Colliery at the top of Lobley Hill bank. I remember going up on the bus with me mam on a Friday morning to collect his pay packet, as he didn't like his cash lying around. He often took us into the pit canteen.

They didn't have showers at this pit so he used to come back home black. Even after he was washed he looked as if he was wearing mascara, the dust seemed to cling everywhere.

Shephards old store draped in 1953 celebration regalia for the Coronation. (courtesy: Gateshead Central Library)

Both he and his father carried the blue scars that pitmen have and wear like a badge of honour. He often used to say that pitmen didn't like to wash their backs because it made them weak. As a kid I was fascinated by his big steel-capped pit boots and leather knee supports. My mam often told the story about my late sister Veronica. She had been quietly playing under the table and it wasn't until the next morning when dad was rushing for work that he discovered she had tied dozens of knots in his bootlaces. He wasn't too happy that day. Later, when I was still little, and he worked at a pit near (I think) Clara Vale, he took me down the pit. It was a walk-in pit and I actually hewed a bit of coal. He frequently took me to see the pit ponies in their stables – Rags was grey with a head that looked too big for him. Jester was my favourite; he was a golden brown and took mints from me.

Maria Thompson

Tommy Lamb, Maria's dad and prior to the days of pithead baths, begins the walk home, dirty from Watergate Colliery, Gateshead, 1951.

Little men off to the pit.(courtesy: Gateshead Central Library)

Pit humour

The last colliery dad worked at was Weetslade at Dudley. Many a time he made me laugh about the humour of the men. There was an Irishman there called Paddy Hatch. One day, one of the pit ponies became wedged by its shoulders in the low roof so the men started digging around its feet to free it. 'Sure' says Paddy, 'don't you know we're eejits, why are we digging around its feet when it's shoulders are stuck?'

Maria Thompson

Pit health

When he gave up the pit my dad worked for a time as boatman at Saltwell Park Lake until ill health forced him to give up this 'thoroughly enjoyable' job. The years of pit dust had caught up with him.

Maria Thompson

Many local cemeteries bear witness to the young men killed in pit explosions.

The Baltic Flour Mills, on the Tyne, where Lena once worked with lading bills. This site now houses the Baltic Arts Centre via the biggest lottery grant ever to the Northeast region. (courtesy: John Johnson)

Shocking

A night that stands out in my memory happened when we were living in Morrison Street, Teams. Me mam and me were, as usual, at the pictures. We came home to find fire engines at the disused pit, which was in a field behind our house. Some children had been playing when there had been a massive explosion. One boy had been killed outright. My friends and I had played there often; it was very much a case of 'there but for the grace of God'.

Maria Thompson

Turnbull's Newsagency

My mam and dad had the newsagent's business in a wooden hut at the end of Saltwell Road, close to the place where the tram came over in the 1920s and killed four or five people. Some thought that our paper shop might be part of the damaged tram; it had one window and at one time included a library. I can remember

there were shelves full of books, and me mam used to stamp the books in and out. The hut was a paper shop at the front, also selling sweets and tobacco, and slightly segregated at the rear was the library bit. They were let out at about a 1d for a couple of weeks similar to another shop on the corner of Rawling Road, Kelvin Grove, that had the same arrangement. When we had to abandon the wooden hut we crossed the road into a purpose-built shop. We stopped doing the library, as I think the council libraries had started by then.

Lena Ireland

At the flourmills

I went to work on New Year's Day when I worked for Joseph Rank's at the Baltic flourmills on the Tyne. At about 10.30 a.m. they would say 'right, ok to go now'. We had worked about an hour. I was a clerk and our chief was a Mr Holtby, he was a good boss. He lived at Ventnor Gardens, Rank's had bought

Sister Gertrude McCormick (now Trudy Baister), is photographed in her nurse's uniform.

Later I moved on to work at the Redheugh Iron and Steel Company down in the Teams district, right behind the Gateshead football ground. It was also next to Davidson's Glass Works. Mr Greens was my boss there.

Lena Ireland

Sister McCormick

I started work at Bensham Grove Nursery School at fourteen. We started at 8.30 a.m. and worked till 4.30 p.m., and had school holidays, so that was great. The children were three to five years. We played games, taught nursery rhymes and sang, and in the afternoon they had a nap for an hour. Miss Craven was headmistress for sixty years. She just died recently [2001], I think she was about ninety.

When I was sixteen and a half years old I started at Sheriff Hill Isolation Hospital, and went to work in many other hospitals during the war years. I worked at Dunston Hill right up to being married in 1949. This was a Ministry of Pensions hospital then and the men all wore blue with black ties as they were serving or ex-servicemen. It eventually became part of the Gateshead Hospital Group in the 1990s. The latter part of my working life was spent between Dunston Hill, Bensham, and the Queen Elizabeth Hospital. I worked in the operating theatre for twenty years before retiring.

Trudy Baister

up quite a few houses down there behind the Ninepins pub, so there were quite a few employees who came up from there each day. We were in the progress department. We were involved with documenting the weights, and checking the quality of the wheat coming off the ships alongside the mill. One of the duties that got me away occasionally was to take the lading bills over to the custom house. This involved a walk along the Gateshead Corporation quay, over the swing bridge and along the quayside in Newcastle to reach the custom house. I would naturally take my time and was in no hurry to leave the customhouse, so I would dawdle and enjoy a leisurely stroll back; no one minded. Another of the bosses was a Mr Wassail.

Grandfather Christie

My Grandfather Christie used to work on the wherries at the staithes (or steeths, as he pronounced them) at Dunston. I remember whenever he wanted to write; he would ask me to pass him the vine.

Mary Davidson

The Team Valley being constructed from fields where Bensham folk once strolled, 1934. (courtesy Gateshead Central Library)

Mr Alberti

I left school at fourteen and went to work down on the Team valley. I went to John Barron's, which made clothes, and my first job was base pulling – pulling the threads out. Then I was put onto a machine making canvas. I moved from there to the brush factory on the valley, but I wasn't there long before I went to Alsco's. It was a good firm to work for. Mr Alberti was manager and well liked, he was a gentleman. I made cardboard boxes here and was on a machine called the 'slotter', and sometimes on a corner slotter. The hours were 7.30 a.m. to 5.30 p.m. with a ten-minute break in the morning, half an hour for lunch and another ten-minute break in the afternoon. There was a canteen and you could order five buns for the week, you paid weekly for these. There was a wireless that played programmes like Music While You Work and Workers Playtime, but it wasn't easy to hear because of the noise of the machines.

I walked to work each day and walked home. I remember the heavy snowstorms, and once losing my shoe in it. Someone at work gave me a spare pair they had to go home in.

Mary Davidson

A little extra

After work I went to the Pal on Saltwell Road to work as an usherette. This got me some extra cash to buy myself a few clothes, as I had to hand over to my mother all my factory money for board and lodging. Mr Scurfield was the manager at the Pal. It was 9d to get in then [1947] – this was for the cheapest ticket in the cheapest row at the front. The high row was dearer because you got a better view.

Mary Davidson

Eldorado

On Wednesday evening I used to go in the cash box. We sold Eldorado ice cream. Choc-bars were very popular then and were fairly new. Sometimes in the evening, after work, I would take some home as a treat and wake everyone up to have it before it melted – no fridges then! They used to all sit up in bed and eat them with relish, they were such a treat and didn't mind being woken for this.

On my night off from the Pal I went to a different cinema, maybe the Bensham or the Coatsworth. We hardly ever missed a film that was doing the rounds and would discuss every detail with our friends at work.

Mary Davidson

Knocker-upper

Willy Woodbine was one of the well-known knocker-uppers who used to wake up all the railwaymen during the night. He never had a cigarette out of his mouth. He used to bang on the door and shout out what the weather was like in somewhat graphic language!

Mary Davidson

Regular tartar

Grandpa Wallace had a red motorcar – he must have been well off then 'cause I had to walk to work and my husband walked each day to Clarkies. At Shephards we got an hour for dinner and had to clock-in and clock-out each time, they were strict on time. Shephards had one adopted daughter, Lila. She married a chap out of the merchant navy who subsequently came to Shephards. They went to live at Rothbury from the Chester's. Her husband and Davidson, the son-in-law, helped to run it for a time. Mrs Shephards was a tartar. I remember one day Miss Graham sent me up to collect some hats and she gave me my tram money to take the hats to Chester's. They started off with a small shoe shop and it grew from that. Marjorie Blair, my friend, started there as well, just before me.

Violet Wallace

Gilsland

Dryden Road was where we used to go for walks; it was all countryside there then. A friend of mine, who lived opposite, had an aunty who worked in Emerson Shephards Store in West Street. Well, she got me in and I was there for about eleven years; I loved it. I started in the millinery department and I went to the classes. We used to have a dance there every year and it was ten shillings – a lot then – but it was excellent. We also had trips. The first one I went on was to Gilsland, I thought it was marvellous. We went in a train, I remember. That would be around 1929. I still get to go to Gilsland with trips organized by the Hardman Centre. We go to the Spa Hotel for coffee. It's lovely there.

Violet Wallace

The cooperage

My great-grandfather and grandfather were coopers. They had the business in Elmgrove Terrace. Grandfather paid for dad to go to Durham College to be a teacher. The story goes that Grandfather Wallace was on his way back to Canada when he met my grand-mother on a vessel en route between Newcastle Quay and London. Aunt Dorothy told me that he wanted to get married and take her back to Canada, but my great-grandfather said, 'if you take her to Canada then you cannot be married.' A compromise was reached when grandfather was offered a job in the family's cooper business. So he

Bensham factory girls at Alsco Cardboard Boxes Team Valley Factory, 1946. The group are: Mary Peggie, Sheila Hannant, Moira Simpson and Rita Lawson.

stayed and married gran. They had a horse but later got a lorry, which, I seem to recall gran called a 'rolley' for some reason.

Some relations in Canada were still in communication with me until recently, when dad's cousin died.

When great-granddad died, granddad kept the coopering business going until he sold it and went off to New Zealand. The house in Elm Grove was in the family for a long time. Last time I looked, the cooperage was in use as a garage.

Audrey Stephenson

Night restriction

You couldn't go onto the main line due to the essential works order then in place. The outcome was that many times I came to work for 7.30 a.m., and may have cycled down from home, only to be told that I wasn't now required until 3.45 p.m. I had to return home, knowing full well that I had to return no later than 2 p.m., as I wasn't allowed to work later than 10 p.m. as that was the law if you weren't eighteen years old. You were sat around awaiting you driver to sign on, for almost two hours. The driver would see you were rostered with him and say 'Fine – I've got a kid on, I'll get a good finish...'

Reg Charlton

In the tank

This made a change to cleaning out the tenders and side tanks of engines. This was a two-man job, and one man was placed adjacent to the lid entry point to stop anyone forgetting you were in there and shutting you in

59

Audrey Stephenson's grandfather at work as a cooper alongside his workhorse in Elmgrove Terrace.

and maybe attempting to move the engine. It entailed cleaning out the dirt that built up in the bottom of the water tanks. You'd be surprised just how many buckets of sludge could be got out of one tank. There were even live fish, and once I got out ball lubricators that must have worked in via the scoop. I could do two big engines in the morning and two in the afternoon plus, maybe, a smaller pilot engine. It took two hours to do one thoroughly as this meant you had to run off all the water for starters.

Reg Charlton

Sleepless

Many drivers due to go to work in the early hours, say three or four in the morning, didn't go to bed when the rest of the family retired as they were too nervous of oversleeping and missing their turn. They would just sit up and attempt to stay awake. Not much of a life, that.

Reg Charlton

Night walking

There were no night buses for shift workers. It was unknown for people to be attacked, many did go out in the early hours to see the last late drunk still careering about the streets attempting to point himself in the direction of home. He was the biggest threat to you. Often, those people who were rich enough to have a car would stop and pick you up, and wish you 'good night', or ask 'are you going to work Geordie?', or 'I'm going over to Newcastle, is that any good to you?'

Things were really quite civil before today's age of drugs and the never-ending pursuit of thrills.

Reg Charlton

Snowball clothes

The overalls where then supplied by a firm called Snowballs, and to this day if I see or hear the word snowball then I think of our blue surge kit.

At first, we were only issued with a jacket. It was blue of course and had the initials

LNER in red on the collar. When I first began, as a lad, my ambition was to somehow scrounge a spare jacket off one of the older men. When you got one you felt you really had arrived. A cap was also sought after and uniform kit was like gold dust.

When I first started my father said 'You'll never stand the shift work Reg – you don't know what you're getting into. You'll never know what time you're starting or finishing – you'll never stand that.'

Reg Charlton

Hours on the railway

In the early days, enginemen had a certain number of hours to perform; it was fifty-six when I first started.

It was true, you never really knew when you would finish and there was a chap employed at the shed simply to tot up what you worked at the time you finally got back and signed off by throwing your check in. You could be called in for eight hours work or other times depending upon how much time you had left to work for your full week. They tried to fit in the smaller jobs for those with few hours left in order to keep down your overtime.

Reg Charlton

Learning the job

The senior cleaner allocated our labours and checked over our work standards for whichever one of the four parts of the engine we had been allocated to clean.

We were each given twelve cloths, and each of the four teams shared a tin of two sections made up of paraffin and Jollip, a polishing agent. We were all enthusiastic and would try to make the best job we could. After a short time, an inspector would question us in order

to see if we were ready to go out firing, which was a big day if he passed you. The aim of the cleaner was, by hook or by crook, to get a cap. So we would ask the old drivers if they had any spare caps and sometimes you dropped lucky. When you managed to get twelve firing shifts in, you got a topcoat, and twelve often took quite a while to get. When you got to be eighteen you could work a night shift. If I arrived at work, and found myself on the daily docket as a fireman, then I would have to cycle back home and re-report at anytime up to 2 p.m. which was the latest starting time, unless you were over eighteen. You might then find that your driver wasn't on until 3.45 p.m. and you had to hang around. If you were down for preparing work, then you were doing this simply for another crew to step in and take the engine off the depot. You would have to check that all kit was present and correct on the loco, which included such things as the monkey wrench, spare gauge glasses, gauge glass lamp, dart, spare shovel, detonators, flags, keys, plus two full oil bottles and a feeder, and there were other items. The oil was got from the store man, who asked you what engine it was for.

Reg Charlton

First journey out

I was with driver Freddy Wall, and it was my first turn away from the shed. We were eventually told we were needed to work a train to Berwick. I said 'I'm not eighteen yet', but he said 'you'll be eighteen when you get back.' I didn't get back until 4 a.m. It was also the first time I got a food ticket. Goodness knows what me poor mother would have thought?

Another crew at Tweedmouth relieved us, and it took so long to get there that I remember the guard down in the fields at one of our many stops, collecting mushrooms!

Reg Charlton

The flyer

About 1932-'33 was the first time engines ran through on the Flying Scotsman. On the first test run my dad was firing to driver Tommy Drummond, and I got to know when it would pass at the bottom of Armstrong Street. I remember it was engine 2544 named *Lemberg*, and it made quite a sight. They said the engine had passed this test with flying colours. Later, when it was quite well established, I continued to go down to the bottom of Armstrong Street to see it pass and give dad a wave. He would have been away from home for two days, as he would go up to London, lodge there, and return on the next down working.

George Bond

First job

My first job was in Shephards store in Ellison Street. I worked in the cashiers place filling the cans with change; these were cash containers, which sent money back or tickets, which most people used then. I had to pull a handle and the canister would wiz along the shop to the right department. My wages were six shillings for the first year, which went up to seven shillings in the second year.

Dorothy Dick

Fishy

I spent a lovely nine years working for an optician opposite the Odeon cinema in Newcastle. It was called Robson's, and as well as making glasses and repairing optical things, they made ships instruments, like sextants, telescopes and barometers. The theatre companies used to

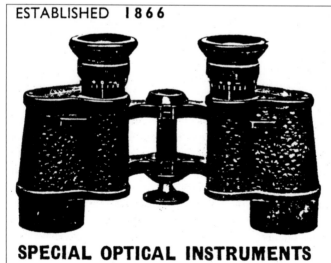

ESTABLISHED 1866

Marine Glasses

Sextants

Thermometers

Drawing
 Instruments

Planimeters

Surveying
 Instruments

SPECIAL OPTICAL INSTRUMENTS

F. ROBSON & CO.

A Robson and Co. advertisement.

come and hire things like lorgnettes, pinz–nez and binoculars for their plays, there were a lot of live theatres about then. The boss was always given complimentary tickets for the show. One Monday morning someone from one of these theatre companies came in to hire some binoculars for a racing scene and as usual left two tickets for the show. The boss, on this occasion, couldn't use them, so he gave them to me and I was delighted. I had a friend who worked at New Bridge Street, so we went together after work. It was a Monday night, the same day that another boss used to get some fish from friends at the fish quay at North Shields, fresh from the catch. This fish was shared out amongst the staff. We all prepared by taking newspaper in, to wrap up our pieces of fish. So I have my parcel ready to take home, but now had to take it with me to the theatre. So off we went and got on the tram from Pilgrim Street to Jesmond Playhouse.

I put the fish against the wall and the seat as we were in the back row. The hotter it became the smellier the fish got, and people began sniffing in the air around us, and looking about. At the end of the play we stood up for the finale of 'God save the King', and I bent down on my knees to pick up the fish. The newspaper was so sodden that the fish flipped and fell all over the place. I had to try and stick little bits of the now–disintegrated paper over the fish, and carry it away over my arms with these bits of paper clagged over it. What a mess, but I was determined I wasn't going to part with it, as food was too short!

I then had to get two trams back home to Gateshead, and when I got off the second Saltwell Park tram, the conductor said 'thank goodness you're getting off this tram with your stink.' How we laughed after the event.

Dorothy Dick

A Co-op store advertisement. Ken and Audrey Routledge both spent their entire working lives with this institution.

Pelaw Mill

When we got married, I got a beautiful quilt eiderdown from the Co-op from all our friends there. It was from the Pelaw Mill, and was a beautiful oyster satin. It was still lovely when I took it up to hand in to the museum staff at Beamish a few years back. We offered it at first to someone involved in the Co-op Museum at Manchester. They said they were interested but never came to collect.

Audrey Routledge

On ya bike

I always loved working with wood and cabinet making. There were some big cabinet-makers

Audrey and Ken Routledge as they are today in 2002, seen with the Geordie Icon as a backcloth on the banks of the Tyne. (courtesy: Trevor J. Ermel)

around Tyneside like Robson's of Spittal Tongues and Neusenboam's on the Quayside. I got on my bike and made enquiries at all I could find. I had all but given up when one night I came back home and me mam says 'There's a letter there on the mantelpiece for you Ken'. It was from the Co-op – 'Start next week', just like that – no further interviews, just start straightaway.

Ken Routledge

Getting your card stamped

After leaving school I had to report every Friday at the Labour Exchange to get me card stamped. It was at the top of Windmills Hill.

Audrey Routledge

Job decisions

I was fifteen years old when I got word that I could start at both the Post Office and the Co-op, on the same day mind! What to do? So me mother and me went down to school to seek the advice of Miss Cowens. She said they're both good steady businesses. I said I fancy the Co-op because the Post Office may well involve funny hours or shifts. Miss Cowen agreed and so it was done. I had made my choice.

Audrey Routledge

Chocolate

Chocolate was about $\frac{1}{2}$d a bar. We would, if lucky, get a bar on the way to school. They were narrow bars I remember. I once got a box of seventy-two 1p bars in a club run at work. We didn't get a discount on Co-op goods like they do now, but the Co-op has been good to its pensioners.

Audrey Routledge

Pension conditions

I did two weeks short of fifty years with the Co-op. You got a £1 for every year. I thought it was hard, but I got £49. A short time after I finished they were paying out in excess of £1,000, but I was really quite happy with what I got. We were made to contribute to our pension from the age of sixteen and I think the Co-op must have been one of the first to insist on this condition. We were like salaried staff from the start.

Ken Routledge

War money

When the war started I was briefly getting more than my father, but he could make good money on overtime that I couldn't. I was on £3 a week in the late 1930s. My starting wage was 10/- a week, it was time and a half for working the half-day on Wednesday. When I left the livery department the boss there stood at the door and said 'Dust tha knaa, I'd have thee streat back.' Which was a compliment.

Ken Routledge

Driving licence – '30s style

In the Thirties you just turned up and requested a licence, no tests or anything, but I just missed that and had to take one of the first tests. It was still very basic and I'm still driving on that same licence today. The first wagons had no windows and I started work on a T-type Ford or a Tin Lizzie. She was TY 7039 – I think a Durham registration. It was very much dependant upon battery power for so much. You throttled up with your hand and you had to rev up hard to generate enough power for the horn to work loud enough to be heard. If you went slowly then the lights faded.

Ken Routledge

Cash car run

I drove all sorts of cars and wagons until, one day, the boss said 'Ken, I want you to drive the private car.' I didn't fancy that as it meant meeting lots of

Greenesfield locomotive shed at the height of its railway prominence in the 1920s. (Kind Permission of Philip Atkins, the National Railway Museum, York)

people, and I didn't know if that was me –
I just wanted the chance to play as much golf as possible at that age. Well, I remember it was the year of the Monte-Carlo Rally. It was great in this big car. Folks thought I was the police, as only they had those sorts of cars then. I started going all around the branches with the cashier. He left soon after and I got the job for myself. There wasn't much security then, for example when I drove down the street towards the branch, the kids along the way would all shout 'Here comes the cash-car'. The people in the queues at the shops would then spread the word along the line towards the staff in the shop 'cash-car's here', and I would beep my horn outside the shop. So much for security, but you could do those things then, it was a different world to today's muggings.

One surly policeman told me that it was an offence to sound my horn when it wasn't an emergency, and he gave me a warning. Later, I would change things and say, camouflage the cash.

Ken Routledge

Skip to work/first job

I used to skip all the way to work. The first time, there was a man on the door at Jackson Street Co-op and he said 'You have to go upstairs to see the boss', that was my introduction to work. I got the job of stamping all the passbooks – there were a lot. Everyone in Gateshead seemed to have one and everyone had to have a book to be able to get his or her 'divis' (dividends). The war ended all of this and everything ended up in change.

Audrey Routledge

Good day – pay day

On Thursday afternoons, and if I was off school and dad was on the right shift, I would love to go with him to the shed to collect his wages. He was a fireman then and I loved seeing the steam engines at Greenesfield. It was a real treat – especially if I was allowed into the cab for a quick peep. It was an extra treat if the engine was getting watered from the big floppy water bag. We would get the No. 54 bus on Saltwell Road to Gateshead Station, and then I would walk proudly up the street to the shed. My dad would hand in a coin-like disk with a number engraved on it, his pay check number, to get his money and he would sometimes look at notices with the other men, all about changes to their rosters. Often I would be given sweets and money from other drivers, or even bits of cake from their bait boxes. My dad had a special white can that he took to work to heat up on the engine to make tea. He would also take rashers of bacon to cook on his firing shovel. I remember he once fell off the top of an engine and sprained his ankle. When I woke up the next morning he had a big white plaster sticking out from the end of the bed.

P. Davidson

Lucky strike

I used to get 2s 6d pocket money that my dad handed to me in his now-empty pay packet. If I was lucky enough to go to the shed, we would go into the little shop on the corner of Wellington Street that sold sweets and my dad would buy $\frac{1}{2}$ lb of Quality Street mix for my mam and a bar of 5 Boys Chocolate for me.

Even when my dad changed over to being a guard when Tyne Yard opened, I still liked to go down with him to get his weekly wages, but modernisation came in the way of a chocolate-vending machine which was very useful and even more convenient! It's a good thing I did continue to help him collect his pay packets or else I would never have met my husband to be, who just happened to be working there as a wages clerk at the time.

P. Davidson

School to laundry

I left school at fourteen in 1939 and went to a joiner on the valley. I was there for three days and my sister went down and told them I wasn't going back because they were using me to heave heavy things about like a mule. Next day I got a letter to say I had been accepted by the LNER and was to start at Greenesfield Sheds on the following Monday. My railway career was to begin in the railway laundry, as you couldn't go on to cleaning until you were sixteen.

My first job was washing all the cloths, but I eventually moved up to become a cleaner and then a fireman. I was with the railway for a few weeks short of fifty years. My first pay packet that I gave to me mam was five shillings. I couldn't enlist because I was told I was in a reserved occupation.

Robert Davidson

Robert Davidson in 1949, seen ready for his next turn of duty on the iron-way as a fireman.

A rude awakening

The laundry was situated off Askew Road, near to where the new signal box is now. When I was working in the laundry at Greenesfield I was given clogs to wear because of the cesspool which was oily and horrible. There was a big powerhouse, a steam engine boiler used to fire this. I remember Mr Garness and Bill Wilson, the bosses. There were pipes all around the laundry and hot-water machines, a bit like those metal containers in a fish and chip shop. They had big belts around and wire netting. The cloths went in and you pressed a button. There were bags on the machines with hot air coming out which pushed the fluff out. You had to go in on a Saturday morning and clean out these bags and get your machine ready for Monday morning.

We used little tablets of soap in the water. There was a machine called the extractor that took all the oil out of the cloths, and this came out into the cesspools. The cloths came from all around the district. There were cloths from York and Leeds and they had to be separated into the areas they came from and sent back clean. There were different cloths for different jobs. The Kitty Brewster's were the heavy-duty ones. We had names for them all. Me mam used to come for me pay packet every Thursday at midday and bring home-made scones for all the lads, you can guess she was popular. I thought the toilets were very strange when I first came to them. They were eight wooden seats in a row, all fixed together and all communally open. You didn't get much privacy I soon learnt, and we each tended to pick different times to go.

Robert Davidson

5 War

'...above all, I am not concerned with poetry
my subject is war, and the pity of war
the poetry is in the pity'

Extract from a letter written by Wilfred Owen.

At the Ritz

When I was a child in the early forties the Ritz cinema opened its basement as an air-raid shelter. My older sister and her friends looked forward to the air-raid siren sounding, as they would grab small suitcases already packed with dresses and accessories, which they then used to good effect doing impromptu concerts in the shelter. We soon found when we were in the basement-end access to the front of the cinema, underneath the screen, a small area like an orchestra pit. We would all sneak in here and, with necks stretched, stand looking up at the screen towering above us.

Of course we would inevitably make a sound and get caught as the checky (male usherette) would hear us and come down to the front, lean over and bawl at us to get back into the shelter.

If the air-raid siren went off when we were at school then we filed into the schoolyard and entered the shelters, which were single-storey brick built with very thick concrete roofs. If we had been hit, the roof falling upon us would have flattened us all!

My mother made me a beautiful cushion embroidered with flowers and a loop with which to carry it. This helped a lot, as the seats were slats of wood on brick columns.

Audrey Nicholson

Tents

We didn't have gardens, so during the summer holidays from school my friends and I used to put a strip of carpet down in the back lane against a wall, then nail an old army blanket to the wall, stretch it out and nail it in between the cobbles. This would make us a lean-to type tent.

Audrey Nicholson

Yes, we have none...

We were all desperate for bananas. When bananas did eventually start to reappear in shops, we still had to use the fruit section of our ration books (1948/49). My mam used to get the bananas and bring back the ration book marked on the back by the shopkeeper, then, the next day, she would spill a little tea over this bit and smudge the section where the tick was. She then sent my older sister for another ration.

Audrey Nicholson

Staff of the Bensham cinema, VE Day 1945. Back row, fourth from the left, is owner Albert Buglass. Second from right is Ernest Brown, the projectionist. (courtesy: Gateshead Central Library)

Wartime

When the sirens went at night we used to go to our neighbours. We lived in an upstairs flat and they lived downstairs. We were put under their stairs, it was really just a cupboard but we felt safe. My father was an air-raid warden. We heard plenty of planes and gunfire. One or two bombs were dropped in Bensham but did not explode, both were near Hendees bakery. Many people were evacuated until they were made safe. I had my appendix out when I was twelve years old and I remember the windows were all sandbagged.

Trudy Baister

Chaos

I remember the schools being closed and the soldiers using them for billets and training during the Second World War. Some people gave over a front room and one of the few teachers who weren't evacuated taught an hour or so each morning, nobody was bothered if you didn't go. My mam did, so I went to a class in somebody's front room in Whitehall Road. I remember Elysium Lane being closed by the police. The mothers taking their children along to Bensham Station and waiting for the evacuation trains to turn up. It was utter chaos. I stood on Saltwell Road watching mothers trying to get past police to take the children home, in the other direction. When the schools did reopen again, Miss James came along Saltwell Road ringing a bell telling everybody the schools would be open on Monday. Only one school opened as it happened, it was Brighton Road, and so one week we attended school in the morning and the next week in the afternoon!

Doreen James

Tea lads?

I also remember the troop train that came to a stand for ages at the bottom of the street. We kids flocked down there and told the soldiers it would be 'quicker to walk mister.' After a while some

Children being evacuated, complete with their gas-mask packs, head for Bensham Station accompanied by friends and relatives, 1939. (courtesy: Gateshead Central Library)

got out to stretch their legs but of course they had to stay near the train. A couple of soldiers started to talk to us girls over the 'batteries' and one bright spark, I think it was me brother, Allan, said 'would yee lads like a cup of tea, cause I can get one off me ma for yers?' The soldier said yes, so our Allan was off like a shot to tell me mam. Well, the soldier and Allan ended up going up to our house and me mam made tea and coffee and in a few minutes all the neighbours were making tea and coffee. Two soldiers carried jugs and cups down to the train, another lot of soldiers carried it on to the train, when they left, every cup and jug had been returned.

Doreen James

A stick-up

I also remember going to Hendees bakery down Lobley Hill and sticking savings stamps on an unexploded bomb. I remember thinking what a waste of money. Sixpence was a lot of money in those days.

Doreen James

Evacuated

One day the four of us were sitting having our dinners in Camborne Grove when this large dark shadow cast a huge cloud across the window. My sister fell off her chair in shock. We found out it was a Zeppelin. We went to Northallerton to be safe shortly afterwards. We had to be placed. We got a right tartar to begin with. We only stayed a couple of months. My husband was teaching down there.

We used to go with the sheep into Northallerton on market day. We loved that.

Violet Wallace

Big bang theory

When we started school, and even though the war was on, we little girls used to walk to school ourselves, but there was one day when we got a terrible fright. We were just walking back from school, a friend and me, and we heard this terrific bang just behind us. We didn't bother look around, but just took off and didn't stop running until we got home. We didn't wait to see what it was. Then Brian came in later and asked 'had we heard?' We said, 'heard what?' He explained that the barrage balloon (that we had seen earlier in the day floating about – after it had got loose from it's mooring) had come down. So we all went back to look, and there it was, its huge big silver skin covering half the street at the bottom of Ely Street. It had also brought down a large wall only about six yards behind us as we walked home. This had been the big bang we heard. There were people killed under that wall. That was the closest I came to being killed during the war years, and it was close!

Audrey Stephenson

Starting out

Where I was born, we lived in an upstairs flat. When the Second World War started I was about three years old, and after we returned from being evacuated, we moved in with my gran.

I remember sitting in my pushchair outside Windmill Hills school and seeing the children getting these yellow ring identities for their clothes. I screamed the place down to have one, so Gran got one and sewed it on.

I remember getting on the train somewhere; it would have been Bensham I think, and getting off at Northallerton. My Granny Wallace came too. Dad came with the school down to Cowton, and I remember we got to this house and an elderly-looking woman opened the door, my gran wasn't too happy there. We got moved onto a farm and I can always remember the farmer's wife doing these enormous Yorkshire puddings. There was also a big gander that wandered around and had learnt to lift the latch on the door. My grandfather stayed in Gateshead as he was on war work at Clarke Chapman's. I later understood that this time was known as the phoney war, and, as nothing happened, we returned after a short time to Gateshead, especially as Dad had also now being called up. He was sent to train the troops how to read so they could follow their instruction manuals, as quite a few couldn't read.

Audrey Stephenson

People

Billy Clayton, later of Clayton & Davies, the ship-breakers, was in my same scout troop, until they moved into a big house on Durham Road. My neighbour was their gardener. He had been in the war as Mr Lodge's batman. He survived the cannon fodder and became a faithful serving man to his old brigadier. That's the way it frequently happened then.

Ken Routledge

Jealousy

Both of our fathers had what they called reserved occupations, Vickers and the Railways. Some people were quite nasty to them and suggested they were having it easy. They didn't realise how hard they grafted and what long hours they did. There was often just enough time to sleep between working.

Audrey Routledge

Ablaze

A bomb fell near Saltwell Park. The theory at the time was that the Germans had seen the moon reflecting off the lake and had thought this was a worthwhile target, but we'll never really know.

I remember when they bombed Manors. What a fire it was. It blazed for days! I remember we all went up onto the Windmill Hills to see the fire blazing. They say that butter and lard were running down New Bridge Street. It's now a cinema complex.

Ken Routledge

Homesick

I was evacuated when I was nine in 1939. I screamed as I got onto the train at Bensham Station because I didn't to go. Even though I was with my sister and two of my brothers, we got split up. I went to Mrs Matheson at Great Ayton and Ina and John went to a Mrs Featherstone.

Mrs Matheson had an outside pump for the water and old-fashioned toilets with just a board across. She was very kind and had a party for me as I was turning ten, but I was only there for two weeks because I was badly homesick.

Mary Davidson

Interruptions

When the war was on we only went to school for half days due to soldiers occupying the school as a training centre. Eventually we didn't go at all and this situation lasted for about eighteen months.

I was fourteen when I left school. I remember my brother, David, throwing his National Health glasses into this huge army water tank on some spare ground near us. My mother was furious and sent me to see the man in charge, to try and get them back. I think she was hoping they would drain this huge tank to fish them out. As usual, being the oldest it was my fault! I often laugh about this now when I come to think about it; me, a ten year old, being sent to ask the War Department if they would drain the reservoir tank to get back a pair of me brother's NHS glasses!

Mary Davidson

Phoney war

Shortly after the war began, the ARP man called up the street, he was a right nutter, he was shouting out 'they've bombed London, they've bombed London' over and over again. Eee, the panic amongst the women along the streets. They thought this was it, they were sure we would all be bombed. All the men were away at work you see, and all the women and children rushed to this little man's house and we all crowded in – I don't know how we all got in. It wasn't so funny then, but I can remember me mam rushing out with odd shoes on – I'll always remember that!

Audrey Routledge

The working man in the Second World War

If my father was laid-off, my mother would know because she would see him coming up the hill carrying his toolbox. The mothers would all say, as if with one voice, 'Oh, they're laid-off.' This sound would ripple through us kids, like an approaching storm. He worked at Vickers, helping to make the tanks and guns that were needed in the war. Eee – I recall in those days he would work all day, come home for food, sleep only a few hours, and return for a complete night shift. How he did it I'll never know. He kept this up for a long time, poor man. His job was mostly standing and it was heavy engineering work. I remember he developed terrible varicose veins – all that standing you see?

David Peggie, complete with those glasses, 1948.

Redheugh Gas Works, 1940. Everyone played their part during the war. (courtesy: Gateshead Central Library)

There were many women employed at Vickers making shells. Even the women with children had to be brought in, such was the demands of war.

Audrey Routledge

Saltwell to Saltburn

We would mostly go to Saltwell Park at the weekends. At the time they were running a campaign called Holidays-at-Home, and so we went to Saltwell Park during the war years. At the start of the war they were going to send me somewhere less dangerous and a friend's aunt, who lived at Saltburn, offered to have me. It was all fixed. Me and me mam went down and when me mam saw the barbed wire along the beaches, me mam said 'she's not going there, she'll take her chance away from a greater invasion threat.' It was difficult telling me friend this.

Audrey Routledge

Shipped abroad

We were told to report back and headed off by train for Annan in Scotland. When we got there a lorry collected us. The driver asked us if we wanted a drink of tea, we said yes, and so he stopped off at a café. The waitresses here told us we were all going abroad – so much for 'careless talk!'

The waitresses were of course right! They were painting over the brasses of the vehicles – we were going where it was hot! I didn't tell my mother until much later.

We were marched from the camp in pitch darkness back to Annan Station. From here we continued through the dark night to Glasgow, and still in darkness were shipped out on vessels into the Clyde, where a large convoy was in the process of assembling. We were sixteen days out into the Atlantic, when one night there was a huge thud. We were all told to 'STAY WHERE YOU ARE' over the PA. Next morning we learnt that the *Windsor Castle* had been sunk, and we later crept into

73

Air-raid wardens, Agnes and Arthur, a husband and wife team, position themselves in an air-raid shelter in Gateshead in preparation for action.

the med. Over on our left, the Rock was in total darkness. Over on the right Tangiers was lit up like Blackpool illuminations! We crept on along the coast until landing, again, in darkness. My transport had been the *Ormandie*. We were told to disembark and make the best of things on the beaches until the tanks arrived.

Ken Routledge

Dig-for-victory

In the war we had a piece of land given by the rector and we all 'dug-for-victory'. There was also another bit of land which we used as the air-raid shelter. I was seventeen when the war started.

Audrey Routledge

Rationing

At the end of hostilities in 1945, every schoolchild was given a tin of drinking chocolate and four apples – a present from the Canadian Government! VE day was celebrated with a street party; every street in Bensham held one, even though many of the adult males were still in the forces.

With the advent of peace, normality returned very slowly as meat, sweets and butter were still rationed. My mam, dad and grandmother's sweet ration always happened to be passed onto my younger sister and myself. The foundling television service was restricted to comparatively few people in London and the Home Counties, thus indoor entertainment centred on the wireless.

Ian Hampton

War memories

Autumn 1940. The sirens had sounded and warned of an impending air raid, and me mother had taken me, a two-year-old toddler, into our neighbour's shelter. We used this particular shelter because it was posh with its two leather car seats, bench seat and bunk. The raid was a big one as the Luftwaffe was targeting the main Newcastle to London railway line that lay at the bottom of Watt Street where we lived. The particular rise and fall of the Heinkel's drone and the crump sound of Big Bertha's exploding shells drowned all other sounds except the whistle that is. I can still hear it now after sixty years as if it was yesterday. The bombs whistle got louder and louder until it seemed to fill the whole bunker. The bomb slanted over the street, missed the railway and fell into Hendees bakery on Lobley Hill Road without exploding. It was defused the next day, I seem to recall, by the UXB boys. After evacuation to Brough in Westmoreland and a return to Newcastle, the bomb was some welcome to our new home in Bensham!

To a small boy, living in the Bensham area of Gateshead meant many things, the result of which fashioned my whole outlook on life; the absence of my father in the RAF, and my uncle, who also lived in Watt Street, was a prisoner of war for almost four years. Another uncle in the Merchant Navy was torpedoed twice during passage with the Russian convoys, and a cousin, aged twenty-two, was killed when the bomber he was piloting crashed in Yorkshire on a return run. My youngest uncle, Jimmy, was killed when his submarine sank in the Mediterranean and yet another uncle was wounded at Arnhem, fighting with the paras.

Muriel Ermel, centre, doing her bit as a land army girl on the Ravensworth Castle estate in 1942.

Drivers and firemen also had to honour the blackout conditions during the war.

Hedley Street boys, 1943

The photograph of the boys [opposite] was taken in 1943. The blond boy in the middle is my uncle Stan Robertson. This is a typical day in the life of Hedley Street when children played in the street most of the day. It is interesting to note the footwear and lack of socks, blackout curtains and the cobbled paving stones.

Ann Jones

Stormy

During the war years most locomotives required canvas storm sheets in place to avoid aircraft seeing a glimpse of the bright fire at night. When I was later in Bomber Command, I would look down and appreciate just why these sheets had to be rigorously in place.

Reg Charlton

These personal tragedies and memories stayed with me during my formative years and I became a great believer in maintaining the strength of the armed forces so that we would be ready if any more megalomaniacs threatened this island.

Ian Hampton

Land army girls

My first job was at the Co-op in Coatsworth Road. During the Second World War the works I was at closed and I was co-opted as a land-army girl. We worked with horses on the land around Pennyfine and the Silver Hills, all to the west of Bensham and across the Team Valley.

Muriel Ermel

Three days on the Iron-Way

During the Second World War, we had some very bad winters. I remember in 1941 (I was now a regular fireman) it was snowing as I set off so I got the tram from Saltwell Park and got off at Gateshead Station. It was a Wednesday. I was booked on the 2.30 p.m. Leeds, with Shire engines then, and the snow was now floating down. After we left the shed we stood for ages on the King Edward Bridge, and it was about 4 p.m. when we got onto our train. Well, when we finally got away after a bit more delay, we were stopped at each signal box to warn us that the telephones where down to the next box. We did this at each box from Bensham to Low Fell and on to Lamesley and Birtley and so on. I felt like I had actually walked all the way to Darlington. At one point, when I had to get out to walk

The Hedley Street Boys, 1943. (Photo courtesy Ann Jones).

up to the box I lost my footing after tripping on unseen signal wires and went down an embankment into fourteen feet of snow. I thought I was going to suffocate, but I somehow climbed out.

We eventually got to York at 1 a.m. the next day. Upon getting to York, control asked if we could work the Aberdonian back, as they had no cover. I said 'hey man, we've signed on 2 p.m. yesterday', 'Well', he said, 'If you wouldn't mind Geordie and go and get some a pie and a cup of tea at the canteen while you wait.' There was little alternative, as this was our way home anyway. We got away from York after 2 a.m. and the route wasn't too bad, that is, until we got to Deerness Junction, when we came to a stand in deepening snow. It was now 8.30 p.m. Thursday evening.

I was eventually told by the signalman (the 'bobby') that five trains were stood ahead but no one knew what had happened to them. We eventually stood there for about twenty hours when the army got through the fields with jeeps and supplied our stranded passengers with hot water, food and milk, to our relief. There were a few very desperate passengers back there. I was subsequently informed that two of the trains up ahead had been forced to throw their fires out. They had ran out of water! Well, we eventually got to Durham station at 8 p.m. on Friday and we got back to the King Edward Bridge at 10.45 p.m. to be relieved here. We had left home 2 p.m. Wednesday and returned home at almost midnight on Friday.

George Bond

6 Leisure

The park is a place for young and old
To stroll around whether hot or cold
A place to spend some hours of leisure
An unspoilt corner of hidden treasure

The park is a place for autumn and spring
To enjoy the delights that nature will bring
Trees casting leaves of crimson and gold
Fresh green buds as they gently unfold

Summer brings families along to the park
Echoes of joy and the song of the lark
Picnic baskets, piled up high
All to be shared 'neath a cloudless sky

Winter brings ice and footprints in snow
People well wrapped with faces aglow
Seagulls screeching over the lake
Swooping down on bread and cake

Outside the world may bustle around
Whilst others enjoy the peace they have found
A sheltered haven to stand and stare
The park is a place for all to share

P.G.

Little Miss Impatience

Dorothy and George had a compendium of games, you know the sort, Ludo, Tiddlywinks etc. which we played on many evenings, and even in my teens we still spent whole evenings playing cards, the favourites being Gin Rummy and Trumps. All we needed to keep going was a quarter of sweets and a pack of cards plus a roaring coal fire of course.

One fairly useless pastime, apart from all the odd-shaped scarves I knitted, was french-knitting. This entailed finding an empty thread bobbin, putting four little nails around the hole and knitting something that just got longer and longer.

The milk-bottle tops in those days were made of cardboard and had a hole in the middle when the piece was pushed out to make a pourer. With a needle we did blanket stitch all around the top and the idea was to do dozens and eventually sew them all together to make up a bag. As usual, mine never reached this final stage, as I left bits of unfinished projects all around the house. 'You wanted to be finished before you've started' me mam would cry out, and I think I have to agree with her.

Maria Thompson

Hi ho silver

We didn't have a television until I was eighteen, in 1961. I think we must have been the last family in Bensham to get a set. If me mam and me were desperate to see something we used to go over to visit my cousin Alan, his wife Mary and their daughter Pauline. Every Sunday I looked forward to *Circus Boy* and for

Saltwell Park maze has always been a great fascination to people of all ages.

a week I used to rush home from school to their house to see *The Lone Ranger*. The radio was still king in our house until 1961 and we were avid listeners to the old soaps; *Mrs Dales Diary*, *The Archers*, *Life with the Lyons*. The radio plays were, and in my opinion still are, very good value, but can scare the pants off you, even now! The first that really frightened me was *The Man in Black*. An overactive imagination can be a scary thing.

Libraries were my other recourse for my imagination as a child. If I could get my hands on a new Enid Blyton story then I was a happy girl. One day I was mortified when the librarian inspected my hands and declared them too dirty to take out a book. I still had to return after washing them, such was my enthusiasm to read.

Maria Thompson

Children's parties

Birthday parties were always eagerly looked forward to – my own and other peoples. There was always money in the scones, 6d if you were lucky. The trouble was you had to eat the scone to get at the money and this left less room for the jellies and cakes. The party games were great as well. Pass the parcel, postman's knock, the hokey cokey, we didn't get goody bags then either and we didn't expect them.

Maria Thompson

Saturday night's alright

We always enjoyed Saturday nights and often went to the theatre, and after the show we nearly always went for fish and chips at Bowers. They had two big rooms here and I liked to sit next to the aquarium. My mam had

Whitehall Road, 1958. Party days were eagerly awaited, and the more the merrier! Some of the guests include Susan Johnson, Linda Burnell, Jean Stephenson, Ann Beattie and Susan Cuthbertson.

a thing about drunks and she would always say 'If we hurry up we'll miss the boozers bus.' It was agony for us if we got on their bus. Our neighbours were always on it and would always bring out their medals to prove that they were Catholics too. They seemed to spend more time in the pub than in the church mind you.

Maria Thompson

Dansette

It was my fourteenth birthday present, my much-loved and much-used Dansette record player. It was covered in green and grey 'leather' and was my pride and joy. It could play 78, 33 and 45 RPM – such modern technology! I had only two records, 'Blue Suede Shoes' and 'Hound Dog' by Elvis. I was heartbroken when

I sat on one and cracked it. That must have been a 'bum' tune said a witty onlooker, much to my tearful displeasure.

Maria Thompson

Gateshead greyhound stadium

Many a time I was found peeping through a hole in the wooden fence around the stadium, trying to glimpse the dogs. My dad found me here once and he paid to take me inside. I loved that.

Maria Thompson

At the hop

I couldn't dance but I wasn't going to let that stop me from going to the hop. Every week my friend Elsie and I would go to the Miners Welfare Hall at Whickham. If I remember right, it cost us 1s 6d to get in and we often walked the three miles, but then we were used to walking.

The band consisted of three or four musicians and one girl insisted on getting up to sing every week. She couldn't sing for toffee! Apart from the rock n'roll I liked the Bradford barn dance because it was the only one I could do.

Maria Thompson

Cycling

I treasured my bike even though it was second hand. It was dark green and it had a guard over the chain. Holidays from school were great because my friend Pat and I would cycle along the Team Valley to Lamesley, what a distance by ourselves and totally free from parents saying 'be careful' this and 'watch-out' that. In latter years, when traffic built up, I got a bit scared to go onto the roads, so restricted my

A dance at St Joan of Arc School in 1953, with Maria and her dad Tommy Lamb.

outings with another friend, Mollie, to the pathway up to Lumley Castle. Having a bike was great but having to keep it wedged in the bathroom was a drawback, talk about keeping coals in the bath!

Maria Thompson

A compendium of games

Rope trick

At Morrison Street we stretched our skipping ropes across the gateposts to make a swing. Mine was fine, but Geordie's on the next gate was too low. As I went to adjust his, Joyce tried to pinch mine and, in dashing back to rescue my swing, I tripped over Geordie's rope, splitting my chin. The scar is a memento that I still carry today to remind me of the 'fun' we had.

Swinging

In Angus Road we were more sophisticated. We swung our ropes across the two arms at the top of the lamppost and swung round the lamp as far as the rope would go, then we'd unwind in the opposite direction. Unfortunately this had its drawback because many a night I went back home sick and dizzy, but of course, it was worth it.

Vogue

Games went in cycles and we played whichever was in vogue at the time. One particular favourite of mine was tops and whips. We used to draw designs in different coloured chalks on the top and it made different patterns when the top spun.

Bays

We used to chalk up our bays on the ground, throw a stone and hop to the particular square in which the stone landed. We had two types of bay; one a square and one circular.

Chucks

I loved the colours of chucks. There were a variety of games to be played with them and each one seemed to be a little bit harder than the last. We played for hours, inside and out. Jacks were similar to chucks except that they were metal and had six arms. For Jacks you needed a small rubber ball.

Queenie

We had group games when all the kids in the street were out. There would be a shout of 'Queenie, Queenie, who's got the ball? I ain't got it, it isn't in my pocket. Queenie, Queenie, who's got the ball?' This would start the guessing as we all stood in a line. Another person would stand in front of us, with his/her back turned. They then had to guess who actually had it, via various clues.

Maria Thompson

Howay thu (Gateshead) lads

Dad used to take me with him to the dogs or to see Gateshead play. It may seem a silly thing now, but the good bit was him getting me a hot cup of Bovril on what was often a freezing cold north-east night. That was living! I was a great Gateshead supporter but missed Hughie Gallagher playing and I think his last matches were before the war started in 1939. I was one year old then.

I do remember the two Callendar brothers, Tommy and Jackie. Grey was in goal. Cairns was number two. There was also Ingham. Our best time was when we got through to the sixth round of the FA Cup, I had to stand outside the Town Hall for ages for tickets. I think it was West Bromwich who put us out on that occasion. Also, on the same occasion, part of a wall next to the Town Hall came down and crushed a lady's leg. I'm sure she was from Saltwell Place.

Although I can't remember seeing much of Laurie at Redheugh I did remember his wife very well, as Ann was in my class at school. We occasionally went to the school sports events together, and I would collect her from where she lived in Coatsworth Road.

Lena Ireland

Roots

The Pal became a car showroom and the spare ground became a garage. Gateshead is still home, even though I now live on the coast. You never forget your Bensham roots.

Lena Ireland

Up for the Cup

Me, Geordie Nichols and my brother-in-law John used to go to Redheugh Park whenever Gateshead were playing at home. You should have heard the cheering when they scored, everyone in Gateshead could hear the crowd, so the wives always knew if you would come back happy or whether you would need cheering up if your team had lost. The supporters used to go down Redheugh in their droves then and we all hated Newcastle United, up in their higher division. Not many people in Gateshead then could even think about supporting Newcastle. Cup fever was rife when Gateshead managed to get into the sixth round of the Cup in the early '50s and we all had Wembley on our mind, plus a little lesson for the great team over the water!

Robert Davidson

Bensham skating rink

The rink was my second home, but was quite small compared with the Tynemouth rink.

The smell, the noise, my friends there with me; the anticipation as I paid my money in for the two hour session; I loved it all. Later I started going to the three-hour session and mixing it with the big boys and girls. The owner was an elderly man, his son gave out the skates and his daughter-in-law sold the light refreshments. Each session I would pray to get a pair of skates where all the wheels went in the same direction – like awkward shopping trolleys today!

I pestered my parents for white skating boots and, eventually, they came one Christmas. I felt like the bee's knees. I then tried making myself a skating skirt out of my outgrown first communion dress, but it wasn't full enough for me; it had to be circular!

One of the men liked to skate with the girls, whisk us around and pull us off our feet. I took great pride in the fact that he couldn't do it to me. I bent my knees, splayed out my feet in a spread eagle, lowered my centre of gravity and he couldn't budge me from this position.

The ring's owner, I think a Mr Johnson, always put on his skates when the music came to the Military Two Step and danced with me; teacher's pet! The sort of things he would tell me when dancing were things like: 'You see Evelyn over there, watch how her toes come up when she puts her foot forward.' He was right, sure enough it did. 'That's not how you're supposed to do it', he would add. 'You're supposed to point the toe and keep the whole foot on the floor.' It did genuinely look much better, and I never forgot his bits of advice.

After the skating boots, the next thing I wanted was a proper skating skirt. I saw this beauty in a sports shop once in Newcastle. It had a full circle, kingfisher blue felt, with black and white rickrack around the hem. I had to have it! Being an only child and possibly a bit spoilt, I got it! I couldn't wait to get to the rink to show it off, as if anyone would be interested, I felt like a million dollars. Now, while I wasn't exactly a Betty Grable I was a bit hurt when a lad called over 'there's better legs on wor dog'. Needless to say I pretended I hadn't heard and skated majestically by with my nose in the air. I was good at doing that! Later on I fell and hurt my knee rather badly so I went home wounded and with a badly-deflated ego. That was not a good night. That little rink is no longer there but I still get a pang, forty-five years later, whenever I pass close by to where it once stood.

Maria Thompson

Park hanky panky

Saltwell Park would capture much of our childhood. Always at some point during the weekend mam and dad would take Judith and me there. We rode the witch's hat, climbed on the monkey bars, and slide down the slide until our legs hurt and our tummies felt queasy. After what seemed like a twenty-mile hike to our little legs, around the lake, we were rewarded with the grand treat of an ice cream, a chocolate flake between us, while sitting by the bandstand listening to the music. Then it was a ride on the No. 53 bus home.

When we were old enough, Judith, Dorothy Coates and sometimes Norma Grey and I would be off to take the park by storm! Daring deeds like fishing for sticklebacks with home-made nets, and jam jars with string handles and, money-permitting, a row in a boat out on the lake, terrified we would fall in and drown as we jiggled around to have a go at rowing.

We'd eat squashed jam sandwiches; drink ice-cream soda, and spy on older couples, some maybe as old as thirty, doing stuff that we would best describe as snogging.

Susan Bulmer

Keeping occupied

Boredom was a word seldom heard when I was young. Complaining about boredom meant been hauled in to wash the dishes, sweep the backyard, fill the coal scuttle or even clean dad's shoes for the morning. We therefore kept ourselves nicely occupied, principally playing with other kids. Judith and I shared a pair of roller-skates and teared down Hedley Street, precariously sitting upon a book that rarely recovered from the experience. I loved a top and whip, and could go as far as Armstrong Street and back to our place in Hedley Street. We would play cricket

Saltwell Park, now the People's Park of Gateshead, has always been a popular spot for all ages in all weathers since Victorian times.

using tennis rackets and a soft ball, hide and seek and knockie-nine-door, until we were caught by an irate parent. We'd also make dens in the railway batteries at the bottom of the street.

Susan Bulmer

Old Ravensworth

When I was small the River Team, or the 'gut' as we locals called it, was a popular place to go for a picnic. The whole of the Team Valley, from the River Tyne to Birtley, was a lovely unspoilt green vale. The children played in the water and made dams. There was also wildlife; birds, rabbits and tiddlers to catch and not far to walk back home to Bensham either. At the Bensham end we also had allotments higher up the hill where cows and sheep grazed. I spent many happy hours there. I can't believe it when I look out of my window, to the west,

and see the factories, shops and masses of traffic in this vista. The only main road to be seen then was the coach road to Ravensworth Castle.

Dorothy Dick

Marches

It was a special day in the year when the Tattoo took place at the castle, with the wonderful sight of the grand finale when all the soldiers with their drums and music marched from the floodlit castle to Lobley Hill Bank and down to Gateshead. Many people lined the route and clapped and shouted as they went past. Everybody seemed elated by it, and it was a grand feeling of camaraderie. It was about the only day in the year when we children were allowed to be late going to bed.

Dorothy Dick

Over the moon

We played 'boody' shops and 'buttony'. You took a handful of buttons and threw them up against the wall. The one nearest the bay used to pick all the buttons up again. We played statues and skipping with a rope across the street. Sometimes we played French skipping with two ropes. We played 'under the stars, over the moon' and used to run over the rope and then jump over.

Mary Davidson

Panto

Mr Jenkins was the headmaster and always wore a dark suit. We used to learn a different dance each week. Johnson's on Trevelyn Terrace was where we used to go on Christmas Eve and get what we needed for Christmas. Today, they are buying stuff months before the event. I missed the panto last year after falling down. This year we're going to see John Inman, he's the Dame.

We looked forward to the Tattoo at Ravensworth Castle, once a year, a trip from school to Whitley Bay and pay a few pennies.

Violet Wallace

Hairy

We used to occasionally go over town and would go on the 'brake'. It was actually a kind of early bus, but that's what we called it then. It was a 1d, or $\frac{1}{2}$d if you walked over the high level. That was a real treat. When we got over town we used to go to the Bigg Market to see the organ grinder, I remember him as plain as yesterday. The monkey had to take the money for the chestnuts you bought for a penny. Oh – they were lovely. There was another man who had long hair right down his back. He would advertise this stuff to make yours grow long – it was years later we found out he wore a wig. The Bigg Market used to be packed out with people. It was a great treat to see these sights for us children. We used to go to Laws (a herbalist) on the High Street for sarsaparilla, have you seen it,

Two little Bensham girls playing 'Boody' shops upon the back stairs, in 1930s gentle sunshine. (courtesy: Gateshead Central Library)

Gateshead Football Club playing in their spiritual home of Redheugh Park on 1 August 1970. This is a pre-season friendly against Brechin. (Gateshead won 4-0). (courtesy: Trevor J. Ermel)

cause it's still there? We didn't get the money they get now, and these things were a treat. If we did get any sweets when out we would have to wait to get them home before we could eat them, stop us dirtying ourselves.

Violet Wallace

That hand

We used to go to the Shipcote (Cinema) every week for 2d to see the 'Clutching Hand.' It was on every Saturday. We used to go to the back to see through the window through a crack, it was a free-show!

Violet Wallace

Falling

We used to go down to the store to see if they would give us the orange boxes so we could get the thick twine off them, we used this to put around the lamps to make a swing in the street. We were always falling.

Violet Wallace

Roamers

I often used to go to Redheugh Park to see Gateshead. I've seen more professional footballers there than anywhere else. You didn't need to stick to your seat, you could roam around the ground, which helped to keep your feet warm on cold days.

Richard Stephenson

Carnival home

Those better off would do yearly carnivals at their homes. One was at Ferdinand's, the bookie, in Marion Street. Everybody went to this one. They were known for putting on a real show with streamers and everything. He always won the prize! Emily Ferdinand was in my class. They would do floats with warning messages on – they did one with a bed on the back and a crumpled bike with a sign 'Teach your child to ride'.

Audrey Routledge

The Gloops

I recall Uncle Nick and the Gloops club ran by the *Evening Chronicle*. It was every Saturday night. Me uncle used to pick me up and sit me down upon the table and get the page open for the Gloops. We would do the crossword competition. I've still got the autograph book that all me friends signed. My dad was a lovely artist and did some lovely drawings in it, so did my grandfather too. Our Trevor scribbled in it a bit but it's still a lovely reminder.

Audrey Routledge

Tyne Bridge relic

My great grandfather had a walking stick. I always remember him telling me that the cane was made from wood from the old wooden Tyne Bridge, and the handle was horn from the deer of Ravenswood Castle estate. All that is left at Ravenswood now is Trench Hall.

Audrey Routledge

Spooky party

We once got invited to a party by a relative of Murray the undertaker. Well, we went to this party and it was in a room just above from all these spooky ready-made coffins. Eee, we played hide and seek around all this lot. The girl's father was a joiner who helped to make them. We had a laugh we had!

Audrey Routledge

Time to waste

There was a space of land in First Avenue on which was built a tumbledown old stone house which belonged to St Cuthbert's church. It became the scout's den. There were three snooker tables there, you used to see all

types playing there, not just the raggle taggles but decent lads who just couldn't get work, this was in the '30s.

Ken Routledge

Risky games

I realise that boyhood memories can sometimes play tricks upon you, because obviously the sun didn't shine every day of the summer and life wasn't permanently a happy one. In fact, some recollections make me realise we didn't always recognise real danger, for example the times we walked from Gateshead to Newcastle along the exterior pipes of the Redheugh Bridge, with nothing between us and the stinking Tyne moving like a submerged crocodile below and waiting for the unwary – just one slip would do it!
Also, the absolutely stupid game of 'chicken' on the main railway line – our pastimes weren't always so innocent and harmless!

Ian Hampton

Don't try this

To youngsters in Bensham during the 1940s and early '50s, sedentary entertainment was provided by the cinema. Our local 'silver-screen' was the Palladium (or the Pal) on Saltwell Road where an upstairs seat cost 9d, with a tanner the price for downstairs. Another 3d bought us a plain Eldorado ice cream. The affluent might obtain a choc-ice for 6d. When we were short of money, which was often, we could get into the Pal for nothing by walking in backwards and the 'checky' thought we were coming out! Only kidding – but one or two DID try this!

Another popular cinema was the Bensham situated at the top of Bensham Road, opposite Turner's the butchers. I also remember going to the following cinemas at various different times: Shipcoat, Coatsworth, Ritz, Capitol, Classic, Scala, Rex, Essoldo, Odeon and the Ravensworth (or the Rats).

As youngsters, our Saturday matinee favourites were Wild Bill Elliott, Johnny Mack Brown – the fattest cowboy hero, Buster Crabbe as Flash Gordon, Fuzzy Knight and William Boyd (alias Hopalong Cassidy). There was also the Three Stooges, and the skinniest Tarzan of them all, Hermann Brix.

Ian Hampton

Saltwell United

Of course the all-time favourite pursuit had to be football. We played day and night with an old tennis ball, as at that time no one could afford a proper Casey.

During winter weekends we played under the streetlights pretending to be Jackie Milburn, Tom Finney and the like. Our basic skills were developed during those early years, playing as we did with a tennis ball in the streets of Bensham. Many of us went on to play for our junior school, and then progressed to various local senior leagues. Three of my friends ultimately played professional football.

This love of football during the early '50s enabled us schoolboys to form our own club, Saltwell United. One of the club members, Alan Simpson, lived in a house with a big clean cellar. It was used as a clubhouse with the permission of his father.

Enthusiasm was endemic, and we collected waste paper and rose hips in order to earn extra money. This eventually enabled us to purchase a full set of blue shirt strips, an infrared ray lamp, smelling salts and plasters. We managed to play our games at the Team Valley, Lady Park or the Mossheaps at Wrekenton. I recall one particularly superb match, when we beat Newburn Manor Juniors 5-4. The club became so successful that the initial membership of fourteen grew

to thirty, and we even had to turn away applicants from outside the Bensham area.

The club also represented Bensham in the YMCA street cricket league in 1952, but under the name of Watt Street, and won the title after a dramatic final game with the runners-up, Carr Hill. I remember we batted first and were all out for 42. Carr Hill came in and looked to be heading for the championship when they reached 38 for 2, then an unbelievable batting collapse followed, and they ended up all out for 41; I had won my first sporting medal!

Ian Hampton

Boys' hobbies

I remember listening to *ITMA*, *Workers Playtime*, football matches and staying up late with my dad waiting for the world championship boxing from the USA. For younger boys, outdoor hobbies and games were the main preoccupation, and as the main railway line was so close, it was natural that we took an interest and became avid trainspotters. I lived almost equidistant between Bensham Station and Low Fell Station. We used to watch the crack trains go along and got to know the best time to be there. We saw all manner of trains, but the *Flying Scotsman* and the streamlined record-breaking *Mallard* were special. It was living, breathing, speaking steam engines in those days and we learned, after some time, to identify many different types – even in the dark – by their different exhaust beats. When I was a little older, I used to cycle to Newcastle Central via Saltwell Road, Sydney Grove, the old Redheugh Bridge and finally the abattoir. This journey was undertaken to enable us to see the 7.30 a.m. arrival from Hawick, down the old North British route. This train used to be headed by a Scott class engine. They were all named after Sir Walter Scott's novels. We saw such as

Saltwell Towers in June 1953. The museum once housed many strange and fascinating exhibits, including an old Victorian room plus sweet shop, stuffed animals and birds, various models of ships plus a penny-farthing bike. Sadly, it closed due to dry rot but is now, in 2003, in the final stages of renovation via a lottery grant to fund work in the Park to return it to its former splendour. (courtesy: Gateshead Central Library)

'Jingling Geordie', 'Baillie MacWheeble' and 'Meg Merrilees'. These engines were an event.

Ian Hampton

Second house waits

I was never far from the cinema. You name it, the Rex, the Palladium (the Pal), the Coatsworth, the Bensham and the Ravensworth (affectionately called the Rats); I've been there. Sometimes the queues were so long that we couldn't get into the first house, so me mam and I would wait until the second house. I used to be so bored standing that I'd count to sixty, then do it sixty times by which time an hour should have passed and so on. I think I must have counted too quickly sometimes.

Maria Thompson

The only watcher

Upstairs at the Bensham, for those who could afford it (1/-), was particularly interesting because at the sides there were double seats, exactly what the courting couples required to get in quickly before they all went. As a child I loved going to the Saturday matinees but it really irritated me that all the other kids made so much noise that I couldn't hear the film properly – it wasn't just when the cavalry came on the scene either! Was I the only one that wanted to hear the picture, I often wondered?

Maria Thompson

Noisy

As a teenager I started going to the cinema every Monday evening with two girl friends.

Bensham Bingo in 1985, which was, in better times, the Bensham Picture House. The swings, close to the Windmill Hills, are where Maria Thompson once regularly played. (courtesy: Trevor J. Ermel)

More often than not we would go to the Bensham, depending on what was showing of course. On the way in we always bought packets of Oxo crisps – four each. Imagine that! Twelve packets of crisps crunched through – now we were the one's making the din! God help the others.

The Rex cinema was rather posh. The curtains were beautifully draped and kept changing colour according to the light upon them. Every week there was a talent contest but I never had the nerve to go up onto the stage. They also had serials, so, no matter which film was showing, we still had to go if we wanted to find out what was happening in the B feature. If I remember it was a Batman film.

'Are you going to the Coatsworth tonight?' Maureen asked me on the bus on the way back from school once. 'Son of Cockeyes is on' she said. How we laughed when she said this. After the tears had been wiped away,

Maureen was told it was *Son of Cochise* and yes, we were going.

Oh those lovely Saturday nights in the 'Rats' with me mam and Auntie Millie seeing Showboat. Those nights at the Horns drooling over the Red Shadow in *The Desert Song*, and many other Saturday nights with our neighbour, Mrs Phillips, when we'd troop off to the Rex, me with me box of chocolates. Bliss!

Maria Thompson

Slow slide

Near the Bensham cinema were the Windmill Hills. The good thing about these hills was that there were swings there. I loved swings, and this brings me neatly to Saltwell Park. Me mam and me often went to Saltwell Park, she would sit and knit while I played. Swings, roundabouts, witch's hat, even a paddling pool in the summer. One day we had not gone prepared for me to go in the pool but I would have to go in of course. Needless to say my knickers got soaked. 'Take them off' suggested me mam. I wasn't very happy at this prospect but supposed that nobody would know. Not, that is, until I went onto the banana slide! Don't you know damp skin is not conducive to a smooth glide, so I proceeded down the slide in fits and starts and made a very jerky and uncomfortable decent, not helped by me mam laughing, knowing what I'm going through. I was mortified and nearly in tears by the time I reached the bottom. To think that people might have guessed I was knicker-less was a lot to bear, or bare!

Maria Thompson

Scary museum

One particular favourite in Saltwell Park was the museum. Penny-farthing bikes adorned the walls, together with long bars of soap and a model of a pit wheel. All those stuffed birds and animals. There was a particularly ferocious-looking wild cat. I was convinced it would come to life, and this scared the pants off me. I remember sitting outside the museum on a bench only to be informed by a friend that I was sitting on whalebone. Well I was up like a shot.

Maria Thompson

Closed station

I loved to walk in the park itself. We had to go along Elysium Lane (Lesham Lane to natives)

and I always branched off, drawn to the entrance of Bensham train station where, to my knowledge, trains no longer stopped. There was a strange attraction about a closed railway station.

Maria Thompson

Sunday walks

We were forever going on walks. Every Sunday we would go along the Team Valley Trading Estate, sometimes as far as Lamesley. As kids we would often go to the Gut (the course of the River Team that runs through this valley) just to see what colour it was that day, such was the muck and stuff that got spilled into it. Can you imagine that today? Every Sunday after Mass me dad would take me to the Quayside at Newcastle. We always bought flowers and put them on me sister's grave in Saltwell cemetery in the afternoon.

Maria Thompson

Pal cinema

Money was very tight and we could only afford to go out separately and took it in turns to visit the Palladium on Saltwell Road (Pal, or fleapit, as it was called) for 9d. A famous character at the Pal was the commissionaire or 'torchy' as we used to call him. If you so much as whispered or rattled your sweet paper he used to shine the torch in your face.

Jean Beattie

7 Body and Soul

'It is impossible to rate too highly the importance of good hygienic surroundings in a town so essentially a "workman's Town" as Gateshead…'

Dr Robinson, medical officer, Gateshead 1880

THE BODY

Dr Naru is a man of multi talents; he has received many medals for his work in dentistry and in 1998 was awarded the MBE in the Queen's New Year Honours list. He is also a qualified Doctor with much experience within various hospitals in the area. His interest in the Arts led to his election in 1975 as Chairman of the North-east Asian Circle created to promote understanding of the arts between different countries and backgrounds. His work with race relations in the area has also been invaluable.

We are proud to have someone with so many great achievements in life working within our local Bensham community.

Dr Naru is very well known and respected in the Gateshead community, for not only his dentistry skills but also for his many other talents. His patients will always tell you about amazing paintings and portraits that were hung on the walls around the surgery.

Dentist and doctor

I came to England in 1952 from Kenya where I was an art teacher. I did my dentistry from 1952-1957. When I qualified, I came to work in Askew Road Health Clinic. Dr Grant was chief Medical Officer of Health and the dental chief was Mr Whitehouse. I would go from school to school checking children's teeth and treating pregnant mothers. While doing my dental work I met George Donaldson who was consultant anaesthetist at the Queen Elizabeth Hospital. He encouraged me to do medicine. I went back to medical school and, to support myself, I went to Mrs Johnson, a very old dental surgeon in Bensham Road next to Dr Chalk's surgery, and started working there in the evenings. This old dentist was not qualified but, then, we used to have Registered Dental Surgeons. She was a very religious lady. Her waiting-room walls were full of stickers like 'Jesus saves', and once she was very upset when someone put more stickers up saying 'Jesus pulls'.

This practice was very old, and I eventually bought Mr Seedat's surgery on Coatsworth Road, Dr Ipatchi used to work there at the time. Incidentally, this surgery belonged to Mr Slater, above York the Tobacconist. It was funny; the same patients followed me to this practice and put a sticker on the waiting room wall saying 'Seedat, Ipatchi, with turban!'

Mrs Humphrey was my nurse, and for thirty years I had Mrs Cora Gordon as my nurse. Without them I could not have done my medicine. We three worked till 9 p.m. at night in the surgery.

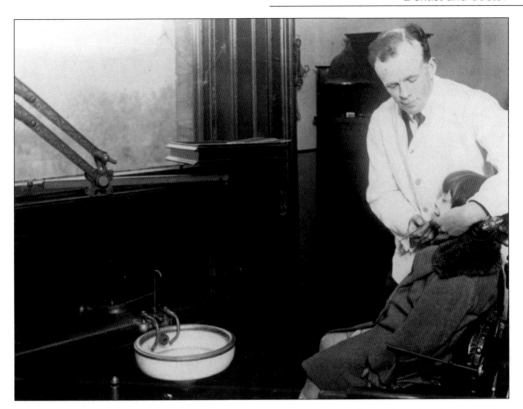

The dreaded Mulgrave (Greenesfield) Clinic in 1928. Its memory lingers on in photographs such as this. Does it bring all the horrors back? (courtesy: Gateshead Central Library)

After qualifying I went to work in the Queen Elizabeth Hospital for Mr Stanley Way. He was a world authority on cancer. While working in the Queen Elizabeth Hospital I continued working as a dental surgeon in the evenings. Many Gateshead people, the local community and the Jewish community supported me. I then moved the surgery to Whitehall Road from where I retired about fourteen years ago. I worked in Gateshead as a dental surgeon for forty-five years. I still work in Gateshead for my son, who took over my practice. I was involved in a lot of community work while practicing.

I came to this country in search of knowledge, but with it I was given so much, that I will never be able to repay my debts to Britain and its people. I have loved every minute of life living here. Every Englishman can teach

A proud moment after Dr Naru had received his MBE.

93

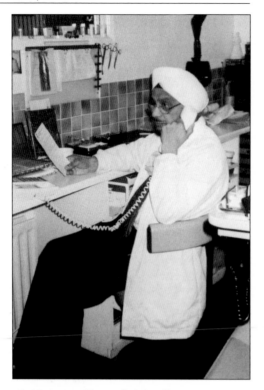

Dr Naru pictured here at the helm of his practice.

and show the world how to live with dignity and honour.

Dr B.S. Naru, MBE

All change

When I had back trouble I changed my doctor because he wasn't very good, as he told me to lift heavier weights! I won't tell you his name, it isn't fair. Someone recommended me Dr Skinner on Whitehall Road, his partner then was Dr Stephenson. They were both good, but very different from each other. Dr Skinner was tall and thin and very serious looking, he also smoked from a long cigarette holder. Dr Stephenson was a well-built rugby-playing type, and always very cheerful. They also had a man called Greenwell working for them as a nurse, he could also dispense medicines as well. Well Dr Skinner didn't take long to diagnose that I had a slipped disk, and was quick to get me fitted up with a plaster jacket for about six months. When waiting in their surgery you had to keep a check on who was in when you arrived so you kept your own turn. This was a bit of a lottery, but if the buzzer sounded and no one moved, you just jumped up quick and hoped you weren't queue-jumping. In later years Dr Stephenson took on the practice alone. He was what I would call a real family doctor and despite his heavy workload would always do a home visit when necessary. He would often take the time to talk and have a cup of tea. He gave a lifetime of service to the Bensham community and it was a sad day for this area when he retired.

Mary Davidson

Synagogue

My doctor was Dr Chalk. He was a well-known Jewish doctor. Whenever he used to deliver babies – most people had babies at home then – he always made a big fuss if it was a boy. He had his surgery on Bensham Road and he was well liked. I think he had a lot to do with organizing the building of the synagogue in Gateshead, so he was quite a busy man in the community.

Mrs Joyce P.

Home remedies

For measles there was sulphur and treacle to bring out the spots. Butter rolled in sugar for sore throats (butterballs). Black bullets steeped overnight in vinegar for a cough. Boiled onions were for a cold. My brother, David, had rickets and used to go to the Sunray clinic for treatment. He did not walk until he was four. Whooping cough was very common then and we were taken out to anywhere where there was hot tar to get a lung full. We were in a doctor's club, which cost about 1/2d per week. Our doctor was Dr Dingle who was No. 3 Walker Terrace. At Christmas one year, I remember him getting the butcher to deliver a leg of lamb to us, as he knew me mam and dad were struggling a bit with eight to feed. There was also a dispensary near the Town Hall. You could see a doctor for 6d, and if you needed treatment you got your medicine there as well.

Mary Davidson

Strange twenty-first party

I had some health troubles when I was about twenty-one (in 1930). The doctor came and said I had to go to the infirmary. My father got the ambulance from Clarke Chapman's to take me over to the RVI. I remember as plain as can be. Mrs Nicklin went with us. I was courting Leslie Cole in those days, and when he came over to visit me they were getting me ready to take down to Walkergate Hospital because they said I had typhoid fever. I was originally taken in because they thought I had appendicitis! Leslie came with me in the ambulance for this transfer. I ended up in Walkergate for three months and nearly had the place to myself. My father eventually went to see Dr Clayton to ask questions. He was the chief medical officer for Gateshead. He told my dad that Walkergate were claiming money from Gateshead to keep me there, to justify the place. They were under no pressure to let me go. Uncle Percy's mother came back with us. I had my twenty-first birthday party in Walkergate Hospital! My mother went over to Carrick's in Newcastle and got a little birthday cake for me. The Sister was lovely. She was a Swede. I thought I was going to be kept in all my life! I can remember endlessly walking around the grounds.

Violet Wallace

The little girl

I have this picture of the one we call 'the little girl' taken about 1900. It seems that a gentleman had lost his wife and needed someone to see to his small daughter. I don't know who had arranged it, but the girl came to my great grandmother. Well, this gentleman later remarried and he wrote a letter asking if little Nora could be reunited with him. My great gran, understandably, hadn't been too delighted, as she was a good little thing, but she couldn't do anything but hand her back. I have here the letter he sent after the girl was returned from his home in Woodbine Terrace. It is dated 14 September 1905, and in it he states that my family were very good to have gone through all of this and the little girl has greatly benefited from her experience with them. We wonder whatever happened to her.

Audrey Stephenson

A recent picture of Violet Wallace.

Norwood Coke Works, Teams, as seen from Bensham streets, 1980. A prime example of a Workman's Town. (courtesy: Trevor J. Ermel)

Home remedies

Chilblains

I remember suffering from the most horrible chilblains. We only had one fire lit in the house, as there wasn't the money for much coal. My mam had her own recipe for the chilblains – it was lard and vinegar. It didn't seem to do much to ward off the chilblains, but the awful smell warded off any one from sitting next to me! 'Snow fire' tablets for chapped hands and chilblains were a more sociable treatment.

Eyesight

I could never see the board at school and had to keep running down to the front of the class to see the words. It was only when I had an eye test at thirteen that they realised I needed glasses. To this day I can still feel the great thrill of putting on those glasses and running around the house, shouting that I could see the bricks in the houses outside!

Dorothy Dick

Smallpox scare

Eee I'll tell you this. Me father, they thought he had smallpox. No one would come near us, and they brought someone up from London. They came and fumigated the whole house and contents, and all the beds were ruined. We all sat outside on the back steps. Well, it turned out it was chicken pox!

I remember them throwing our schoolbooks

along the passage in a heap, it was terrible. They took dad away in a car with a rug over his head to the fever hospital up Sheriff Hill. He had a marvellous time because he wasn't really ill. He had a ward to himself, and all the nurses that came with it! I cried when my dad was taken away and my granda came and took me out to buy some real chocolate. The only kindness shown to me mother was an old lady who lived across the road from us. She said to me mam 'Oh Lizzie love, don't fret, I'll wesh ya weshin for ya'. Me mam never forgot that kindness. Everything had to be washed you know, everything!

Audrey Routledge

Going to the doc

We seemed to be forever going to the doctors. In one door was what looked like a church pew hugging three walls, and another door out of which people disappeared from time to time, and that was it!

We didn't have to ask who we were following in, 'cause when someone went out of the second door everyone shuffled up, and you kept doing this until it was you next for the door. The seats were well polished by Gateshead bottoms!

At Dr Chalk's you went in and said 'who's last' and you then knew who to follow. I often think of that austere waiting room when I drive past St Cuthbert's church today, as it was just opposite.

Maria Thompson

Davies and Omroid?

There were two doctors in the practice; I think they were Doctors Davies and Omroid. The practice was at the Teams, near the bottom of Askew Road, in Johnson Street.

Maria Thompson

Cartwheels

I can remember when I was about four, standing in the queue waiting for the doc's door to open, and I just started doing cartwheels out of boredom. I became the entertainment for the all the queue. Such a young show off me!

Maria Thompson

Chalky white

Because my dad's doctor was Dr Chalk on Bensham bank, my mam decided that we would join that practice instead. Dr Chalk frightened the life out of me for the simple reason that he was deathly pale and rarely smiled.

Maria Thompson

Strip search

One of the most dreadful things for small girls was having to strip off to your knickers and vest, or liberty bodice, in the freezing cold surgery. If there was one thing worse than stripping off it was the foul-tasting medicine resulting from that visit, especially that horrible purple stuff.

Maria Thompson

The big hospital

I had to go to the big hospital, the Queen Elizabeth, to have my tonsils and adenoids out when I was six. I went in on a Sunday afternoon and the ward seemed huge. There was only me and one other child in the ward, the rest were adults, I think. Anyway, there was a smashing dolls house at my end of the ward and, do you know, I never managed to get my hands on it.

I remember vividly the smell and horror of going under the gas and kicking my legs madly, a

'The little girl' is pictured below, fourth from the left hand corner, on a seat at the back.

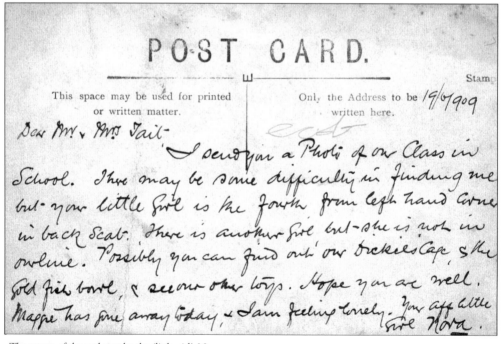

POST CARD.

This space may be used for printed or written matter.

Only the Address to be written here.

Stamp

19/6/909

Dear Mr & Mrs Tait -

I send you a Photo of our Class in School. There may be some difficulty in finding me but your little girl is the fourth from left hand corner in back seat. There is another girl but she is not in outline. Possibly you can find out our Dickies Cage, the Gold fish bowl, & see our other toys. Hope you are well. Maggie has gone away today, & I am feeling lonely. Your aff little girl Nora.

The reverse of the card sent by the 'little girl' Nora.

Dr Stephenson relaxing at home with his dog after a busy day.

fight I was doomed to lose. The next memory is of being sick all over my bed, as the nurse didn't get there in time with the kidney disk. I also recall being given a dish of water, some soap and a flannel and having to wash myself sitting up in my bed. The little boy opposite would not wash himself and I, such a prig, said to the nurse 'he's naughty miss.'

Maria Thompson

Greensfield Clinic

I still shudder when I pass this place, so dreadful are the memories of those in white coats who worked there. There was terror of going under the gas, the loud buzzing in my ears, all this to find, when I woke up, that they had taken out the wrong tooth. They wanted me to go straight back under again but me mam wouldn't let me, thank goodness.

When I was very small I went here for sunray treatment. There was a very distinctive smell in the room and we all stood round in a circle wearing only knickers and green goggles.

Maria Thompson

Dr Stephenson

Doctor G.P.G. Stephenson MB BS was born 24 November and died 22 July 1996. He qualified on 9 May 1943 from Durham University and went to Shotley Bridge Hospital before going out with the Armed Forces to East Africa where he was eventually to serve as a major in Kenya and Uganda.

When he returned, he did part-time Medical Boards for the MOP and continued to do Boards until retiring at seventy.

He joined Dr Skinner's practice at No. 170 Whitehall Road, where he remained for twelve years before starting out on his own at No. 140 Whitehall Road. Here he practiced until retiring on 30 June 1987.

He did over 1,000 post-mortems whilst filling in for his father, George, who was a Home Office Pathologist and Police Surgeon in Newcastle. I always remember him saying that it was not how people died that amazed him, but how they ever lived with so much wrong with them!

He had many interests; archaeology, antiquaries, rugby and was a keen philatelist.

He was also very fond of animals and Mrs Bryson made him a Life Patron of the Northern Counties Horse and Small Animals Protection Society.

He worked hard all through his life, was kind hearted and was very fond of all his patients. He knew them all extremely well and they seemed fond of him.

Mrs Sylvia Stephenson

THE SOUL

On that first morning I came down to the Mission I knew no one in Gateshead. There were no workers, nothing but an empty and rather dilapidated building. I just knelt down in the bare hall and prayed 'Heavenly Father, you and I can do this work. Show me where to begin.'

Sister Winifred

The Almonds

In those days after having a baby you were not allowed to go into anyone's house until you had been 'churched' and the baby had been christened. It was considered unlucky and people were very superstitious. When you had the christening you always put up the christening bread, which was usually a teacake with cheese and money in the middle. If it was a baby boy the christening bread was given to the first little girl you met on your way to church. If a girl, then it was given to a little boy. The very first house you took your baby into after being christened gave you the almonds – these were candles, matches and money, meant to 'light your way to heaven.'

At weddings there was the 'hoyoot'. The wedding car with the bride and groom threw money out of the car window and the watching crowds would scramble for the coins. Some kids used to find out where all the weddings were to make sure they were in a good position. Cars were booed if they didn't have a hoyoot!

Mary Davidson

May processions

I always looked forward to walking in white. I liked nothing better than getting dressed up. Some of the very poor families couldn't afford the white dresses and the teacher always said it didn't matter, but I used to be so glad I wasn't one of them. My dad would buy me flowers from the Sunday quayside to carry in the procession.

The priest would wear rich golden robes and the alter boys would carry the statue of Our Lady around in a shallow box with handles, rather like a sedan chair. The box was always full of flowers too, it must have been quite heavy. She often wobbled as the boys carried her, shoulder high, and I was always on edge in case she tipped over. She never did, probably divine intervention. My mam and me liked to go to St Dominic's church in Newcastle for their processions because theirs were always a bit more spectacular. Then afterwards we would walk home along the banks of the Tyne.

Maria Thompson

Church

I always looked forward to St Patrick's Day because we ere given a piece of shamrock to wear, and beside, I liked the hymn singing 'Hail Glorious St Patrick...'. Ash Wednesday wasn't so good 'cause I always felt stupid walking around with a grey thumb print on my forehead. I used to rather irreverently pray that it would wear off quickly. I was perhaps not martyr material!

Maria Thompson

First Holy Communion

In the '50s we had to fast all night before taking Holy Communion. No wonder people were always fainting. The rules were relaxed in latter years.

It was very exciting getting all dressed up in white; dress, shoes and veil. Because we had all fasted, we had a breakfast party in the classroom afterwards, a paper bag full of buns and cakes – just like at our school Christmas parties.

Maria Thompson

Sister Winifred

She was a sort of religious lady, like a nun but not quite the same. She wore the same coat all the time. She also had a hat with a broad band of striped ribbon around the brim that then cascaded down her back almost to waist level.

Maria Thompson

Banners high

The 8th Gateshead Girl's Brigade would meet up in the Trinity Church Hall every Thursday. There we would learn to march, shoulders back and heads up. We were drilled army-style until we could do it with our eyes shut. On Remembrance Sunday in November we would march with our banners high along Alexandra Road to the war memorial. The brigade taught us first aid, teamwork and basket making. It was hard work but also good fun.

Susan Bulmer

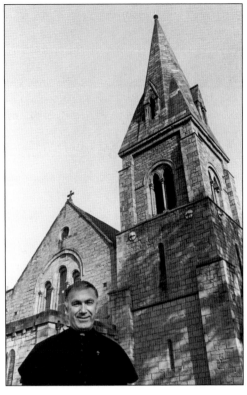

St Cuthbert's church, Bensham Road, with Revd John Parker. Sadly, the church closed and was a subject for vandalism, but it may yet be re-opened in the future as an active church for another denomination. (courtesy: Trevor J. Ermel)

The little Sister

I can remember Sister Winifred bustling up and down the street when I was a little girl in the Teams. Of course I didn't realize then how special she was, because she was such a familiar face in my childhood and everyone else knew her and spoke to her. I went to the mission before I moved further into Bensham and I remember the mission songs we sang and how everyone spoke about Sister Winifred with the greatest respect. She was a lovely person. I don't think she was very big but she did have a presence about her. I suppose you could say it was radiance.

Mary Davidson

Two Jewish boys taking a stroll and a welcome break from studies near Prince Concert Road.

Jewish friends

I had quite a few Jewish girls in my class at school. Some were from Germany and some from Russia. I was always envious that they could leave school early on Friday so that they could get back home for their Sabbath-day preparations. A Jewish lady owned our flat and we had to pay rent to her. I remember my father rushing to her house with a loaf of bread, which had burnt in the oven as it was so decrepit. I remember this being a disaster as this was our main food that day. Eventually the oven was replaced!

Mary Davidson

Water hole

We were fascinated to watch all the Jews walking down to the Team Gut every year for one of their religious occasions which required them to be near water. Sometimes we would be asked to turn a light on or off on a Saturday, as they weren't allowed to do this as it constituted work.

I remember how all the Jewish girl's seemed to have lovely black curly hair and wear lovely smart clothes for school.

Dorothy Dick

Jewish wedding

When I went to the grammar school it was the first time I met any Jewish girls, as none went to my primary school. I admired their strong family ties and traditions and, through my Jewish friends, I became involved with their families who eventually asked me to baby-sit for them. I used to live near the Jewish community, at the top of Whitehall Road. Once I was invited to a wedding which was held in a garden in Bewick Road, and I thought it was so beautiful with a canopy and lots of singing from the men as they joined together dancing down the street. The shops on Coatsworth Road where I shopped were always very busy on a Thursday in preparation for the Sabbath, and we used to be able to buy Jewish New Year cards from the Post Office to give to our friends.

Mrs A.M.

Merry dance

A group of us girls from Brighton Avenue School used to go to Girls Brigade, which was led by Mrs Aisbitt and Mrs Douglas. Mrs Aisbitt had a daughter, Valerie, and another girl called Margaret Hetherington who used to help. We used to lead those poor girls a right dance during the marching as we would bump into each other deliberately and giggle. We must have done something right though, because we were entered into marching competitions and gained many badges which were sewn onto the sleeves of our black tunic uniforms. Despite our high spirits I'm sure we gained something from our Girls Brigade experiences.

Mrs A.M.

...with paper

I went to Sunday school at Rawling Road Methodist church. Mary Thompson, who was a probation officer in Gateshead, ran it. I was about two or three when I first started, and I remember it was a little room with a piano and the hymns were on a roll, which I think was some sort of cloth. It was turned over for the different hymns. We sang 'action' songs and had a story, then we went into groups and coloured in pictures in a leaflet we were given. Every year we had a church anniversary when everyone sat on little chairs on an erected stage and said a little piece of poetry, which we had learnt by heart. One year sticks out in my memory from the rest 'cause I shouted down from the stage to my parents to tell them I wanted the toilet. They tried to beckon me off quietly but I think stage-fright had set in because I next shouted '...with paper.' I'm glad video cameras hadn't been invented in the 1950s!

P. Davidson

Gran's finery

We had church outings to Tynemouth, and harvest suppers, and I would often go on the pensioners' bus for their mystery trip with my gran. My gran loved her pensioners meetings and this was one of the times when she

Lawrie McMenemy and his bride, Anne, on their wedding day at Corpus Christi church, Bensham. Also in the view Lawrie's younger brother Paul. (courtesy: Evening Chronicle*)*

adorned herself with her false teeth and Sunday-best hat and, complete with glasses, she would stand up and proudly sing 'onward then ye pensioners' in all her finery. She also liked to keep a look-out for the then minister, Mr Jex, whom she thought rather handsome. Rawling Road Methodist church changed its name several years later to Trinity Methodist when it merged with the 'tin-chapel' further along Rawling Road near Faraday/Rayleigh Grove.

P. Davidson

Trinity Methodist church, Rawling Road – now a doctor's surgery, saving bodies rather than souls.

Deadly phonecall

I can remember when the vicar was killed. He went to make a phone call and whilst he was in the box a runaway lorry collided with the box and he was killed outright. The vicar of St Edmunds was Canon Stephenson.

Violet Wallace

The family Sunday

St John's church, Dunsmuir Grove, was my second home. It was a congregational church that had started off in the upstairs room above Kelly's printing works, on the corner of West Street and Ellison Street. A church was built near Windmill Hills and my father, Richard, was senior elder, two of the other elders were Dick and Harry. You can guess what their collective name was. Then they built the Dunsmuir Grove congregational church. When the church was later sold, everyone moved to the church that was built on Cromer Avenue. My father had an allotment on the land next to the church.

Dorothy Dick

Scouts / Guides

In Brownies we used to go along the Team Valley, before it was built on of course, to complete tests to get our badges. We had to make a fire and boil an egg. We did this near Low Fell station. There were tennis courts down there as well, by the Methodists. They were quite expensive for a game I seem to remember.

Audrey Routledge

Sundays

When I was little I would go for a walk with my granddad, every Sunday, to put flowers on me gran's grave in the cemetery. We would then go for a walk by the turnip field, which was alongside Dryden road then, its now all houses. My other gran lived opposite the chapel where we went before our walk, every Sunday. To live near the chapel was the place to be. All the councillors and the mayor attended this chapel. We even had Mayor's Sunday, for this everyone went. The Magnay family also went regularly, he was our MP. I remember their son was a solicitor. When I went into the forces, he would always say, 'come to the Houses of Parliament, any time, and I'll take you through.' When I did have a chance, my friend said 'I don't believe this', and wouldn't come. I always wished I'd just gone.

My other granda did stonework, he was a mason, and he did the portico stonework at the central station in about 1848. He eventually died young due to the dust of the job getting on his chest.

I went to chapel as soon as I was three, and one year I remember I got a prize. It was a first aid kit, which did not thrill me!

Audrey Routledge

Churches – when I was four

Another colourful character was the Deaconess from St Chad's Parish church, who walked up and down the street a lot in her navy uniform and hat. I was so impressed by this that I stopped and asked her if I could come to her church. I think I rather liked the idea of becoming a deaconess and being able to go up and down the street in a uniform and hat.

Two Sisters who were regular attendees at this church used to walk up and down the street on a Sunday. One of them used to fascinate me

Gateshead Boys Brigade, mid 1970s. Courtesy Gateshead Library.

because she wore a fox fur around her neck, which I did not like the look of. One day I told my mam that I did not like this ladies 'Davy Crocket hat'. I never liked anything made from fur since that time – maybe that's also why I'm a vegetarian today!

P. Davidson

Bats in the belfry

I did in fact go up to the Sunday school morning sessions for a few months at this same church as well as attending my original Methodist Sunday school in the afternoon. My parents would no doubt have taken full advantage of the bit of peace this gave them! At St Chad's you were given a lovely sticky Bible picture-stamp to put on a card each week, and I remember the strange aromatic smell from the burning of frankincense. This church also had a clock in the tower with bells that chimed each hour, only sometime the bells would go off at other times, I found out this was caused by pigeons and bats in the tower. It was rather a 'high', church leaning towards Catholicism and it had a large crucifix near one of the doors. My friends and me used to take up pieces of bread in case Jesus was hungry. We were amazed to find them gone next time we went in. Jesus really did eat them we thought. As well as a crucifix it was a grand church to play in at weddings as it had a porch area with lots of stairs going up, and open windows rather like a castle. This was perfect for playing Robin Hood type games which included a tragic Maid Marion scene and much shouting from the little windows along the lines of 'save me, save me' which must have gone down well with the clergy inside!

P. Davidson

Dances

Church loomed large in my life. We had to have mass in the school hall because we didn't have a church then. We had smashing church dances too. My mother was always on the cloakroom and helping her was almost as good as going to the dance itself.

Maria Thompson

Good manners girls

I spent many happy hours at the Girl's Brigade at the church on Rawling Road. I used to walk up Whitehall Road and call on my friend, who would be waiting for me in the pathway fully kitted out in uniform and complete with subs money. I remember working for my Duke of Edinburgh's award and going to the hall opposite Brighton Avenue school to set up the room for a coffee afternoon, and placing the tableware in the correct position to pass 'good manners' for the bronze award. I also remember the ten-mile hike while we were at the Biggar Brigade and camp in Scotland. It was freezing in the tents, especially during the night and early morning. This didn't deter our enthusiasm for eating the sweeties we'd bought earlier from the tuck shop, after lights went out, and listening to tales about the Boy Scout's who were in the field next to us.

Anne Jones

Spinning chair

Being a Methodist church we saw many changes in minister at Rawling Road (later to become Trinity) Methodist church. I can vaguely remember Mr Jex being there when I was little. Mr Bowes was a lovely young minister, who came with his wife and family, and then there was a Mr Candiland. He was a very thin, tall, angular man and he could not

The war memorials near Shipcote. Susan marched here on Remembrance Sunday with the Brigade.

keep still when he was in the pulpit. He was always spinning something around with one hand, such as a chair, and he had everyone sitting on the edge of their pews waiting for the object to topple. I wonder how many people can remember him?

Then there was Mr Estelle, who was known to preach a good sermon and Mr Pratt who was a middle-aged gentleman, with a liking for the old Chatham and Dover Railway Company, and he could speak fluent Chinese. As well as conducting my wedding Mr Pratt also baptised my elder daughter.

P. Davidson

CERTIFICATES

This is to certify that

ANNE BEATTIE

having satisfactorily observed the conditions of training and reached the required standard in each section, is now qualified for the following Award.

Bronze Award   The Girls' Brigade

Brigade House,

Authorising Official   Parsons Green,   Telephone

Appointment   London S.W.6.   Renown 5461

Organisation   Brigade Secretary   *Irene Haworth*

Date   *11th November, 1966*

40

Anne worked for her Duke of Edinburgh's award at the Girl's Brigade, Rawling Road.

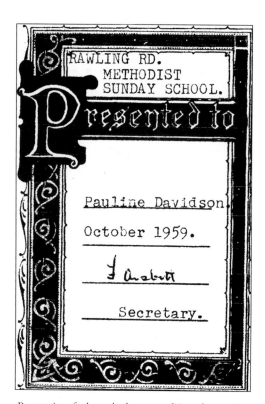

Presentation of a hymn book was a tradition when moving Sunday school departments from primary to junior.

Bodies not souls

Mr Aisbitt was church secretary for many years and he was well known for always singing rousing hymn choruses wherever he went (I'm told even at his workplace). Mr Feetham was a well-recognised character on a Sunday and seemed to do a lot of the organizational jobs.

When the congregation began to dwindle, the church sadly closed its doors and the faithful had to go up to the church at the top of Whitehall Road, on the corner of Coatsworth Road. After closure it became a doctor's surgery and took on a new role saving bodies rather than souls.

P. Davidson

8 School Days

'In addition to the basic subjects, the master had to be prepared to teach to all the children of the parish of Gateshead, the Latin and Greek tongues; as also write and cast up accounts, and also the art of navigation or plain sailing'.

Courtesy Frank Manders, *History of Gateshead*

Brighton Avenue school

I went to Brighton Avenue school in the early '50s and I can still remember some of the teachers there. I think the headmistress was Miss (or Mrs) Knight. There was Mrs Matheson, the baby teacher, she took the new starters at five. There was also Mrs Watts and Mrs Clough, who were lovely. Mrs Brewis, who I also liked, took another class. I always wanted to be Mrs Brewis' class but I was put into the top class with another teacher who I didn't like. I think she was called Mrs Robson. We had a weekly test and were put into seats depending upon our class positions, starting with the cleverest at the back. She also gave out 6d to the person who was top. It was usually the same girl who got that week after week and she was also the teacher's pet. Then my moment came and I made the top spot, and guess what, she decided to stop the 6d prize money, I thought it typical of her. I remember the top boy dirtying his pants one day in class. I do know his name but I won't tell you as it doesn't seem fair, especially now he's a vicar!

Dinners were served in the school hall. At dinnertime we would sit at long tables with a teacher at the top. The headmistress would come in to sing grace before we ate. She would say:

Thank you for the world so sweet
Thank you for the food we eat
Thank you for the birds that sing
Thank you God for everything

She would start off for this song with a high-pitched note, and one day I just had to let out a huge guffaw as I thought it sounded so funny and I was told off. My mam also made me apologise to her the next day. The meals were brought in from outside by a van and were in big steel containers like huge tureens. I loved the runny-pease pudding but hated the lumps in the custard. We all loved the chocolate pudding with pink sauce.

Mrs A.M.

The Red Hand

The outside toilets were a nightmare. They always seemed to be frozen or something, and to make things worse the bigger girls told us that one of the toilets had a red hand that came up out of the pan, so we were petrified to go in, in case it got us.

In the Junior school I remember a Miss Dumler (her parents had a pork shop) but the teacher I remember best was Miss Bourne,

MEMORANDUM.

Gateshead Education Committee.

FROM

Brighton Avenue school.

Boys' Department.

July 21 1939.

TO

Whom it may concern.

EACH communication should refer to ONE subject only.

Robert Davidson, of 25, Stevenson St is leaving this school at 14, having reached standard 5A in which he has been my pupil since August 1937. During that time he has impressed me particularly with his perseverance & honesty. Whatever his limitations in purely scholastic work he has never ceased trying & has always been most helpful & obliging.

His general attitude has always been most respectful & I am sure that he will be successful in any position in which his willingness and obliging qualities are of use.

I shall be glad to answer any inquiries.

Thomas A. Bell.

B.Sc., D.Th.P.T.

Robert Davidson's school reference given to him upon leaving school in 1939.

Form 1B at Gateshead Grammar School for Boys in October 1962. This was the final term in the old school building before moving into the new one. Trevor Ermel is second from the left in the middle row. Other names are Alan Carrott, Michael Ball, Ian Smith, Tommy Dobson, John Reed, Peter Crisp, Brian Cook, William Atkinson, David Mitchell, Robin Corbett, Alan Sergison, Tony Yates, John Wildsmith, Mr Addison (form-master) Neil Hepple, Leslie Milne, Frank Moon, Ian Robinson and John Pears.

Brighton Avenue School, 1938. Mary Davidson (née Peggie) is seen in back row on the left — nearest the wall.

Bensham Grove Nursery School, 1929. This historic corner was the home of the first nursery provision in Gateshead. These children would be some of the first to use this facility. Courtesy Gateshead Library.

she was everybody's idea of the perfect teacher. The girls all wanted to be like her and adored her; even the little boys cherished her. I think everyone cried when we left that class.

The Junior school was closed down and everyone had to go along to Kelvin Grove school, so then there were more tears. When we went to Brighton Avenue we used to go over into the Presbyterian church hall for the dancing. It always smelt peppery and I never found out why. We were all taught country dancing and dances like the Gay Gordon and the Military Two Step.

We were taught folk songs, such as Early One Morning and The Keel Row. We didn't have things like the National Curriculum then, but we had respect for our teachers and a good all round education (and on a low budget). Somehow the teachers then always found time for that all-important end of day story that took you far away into another world.

Mrs A.M.

Bensham Grove Nursery School

I went for an interview at Bensham Grove Nursery in April 1972. At that time teachers applied to the Local Authority and were then sent where there was a vacancy. Although I had already been offered a job at Harlow Green Infants I really wanted to work with younger children, so I was keen to see this nursery. Although born and bred in Gateshead I wasn't very familiar with the Bensham area then.

It was a lovely spring day as I drove towards the school. I did know about Bensham settlement and the many courses they offered for evening classes, in fact I had been involved with a pottery class there, but I hadn't really taken much notice of the surroundings as it had been dark. I was a bit disappointed by the dirty back lanes where I had to leave my car, and couldn't believe I had come to the right place as I struggled with the high wooden gate within the even higher fencing. So you can imagine my surprise to find on the other side a modern building surrounded by neatly trimmed grass, trees, a clean and tidy sand pit and climbing frames, and to hear the sound of children happily engrossed in their play.

E. Burn

Mammy hungry

My memories of Bensham are some of my happiest. I felt I was able to give some children a little bit of respite away from the outside hustle and bustle. Sadly, many of these children came from unhappy backgrounds, but this was not always the case. I can remember finding one little boy in floods of tears and when I asked him why, he said 'I'm just hungry for me mammy'.

I've always treasured this as one of the best expressions of love I've heard. I will always

have fond memories of Bensham and it's good to know that the good work goes on at this location. It is a very special place because this was the first nursery provided by the Gateshead Education Authority back in 1929.

E. Burn

The Bishop's visit

During the 1970s I was a teacher at St Mary's Church of England Infants school in Gateshead. It was a small school at the bottom of Windmill Hills with a lovely view over the River Tyne and Newcastle beyond. A favourite pastime on a clear day was to spot some of the well-known landmarks over the river. The lantern tower of St Nicholas' Cathedral, which the children thought looked like Sleeping Beauty's castle, was one. I still think of this vision today whenever I cross over the Tyne Bridge.

Staff room at St Mary's Church of England Primary School where Pat Warburton (seated left) taught for many years. St Mary's was the oldest school in Gateshead, but has since closed.

The school was the oldest in the Borough and as a Church school, apart from the regular visit of our rector, we would occasionally be visited by other members of the Anglican hierarchy. One such visitor during my time there was the Bishop of Durham, Dr John Habgood. I still remember clearly the morning that he came. The children had all been told that an important person was coming to see them and that they were all to be on their best behaviour.

When the Bishop came into the classroom – I remember he was very tall and had a quiet, kindly demeanor – he asked if he could just walk around and chat to the children. So, without ceremony, he went from table to table, bending down to the children's level to talk to them.

When he reached the last table I noticed that one little boy seemed to be entranced by our notable visitor. In fact he couldn't take his eyes off the Bishop's decorative cross, which hung around his neck and was glinting as it caught the sunlight. He ultimately burst out with 'Mister, I like ya necklace'. 'Do you?' smiled the Bishop, 'I am glad'.

What the Bishop did not know was that after he had gone this incident led to an impromptu class discussion about the cross and its significance. I'm sure the Bishop would have approved!

Mrs P. Warburton

School years: Kelvin Grove

I came to live in Saltwell Road when I was almost eleven years old. I went to Kelvin Grove School in the seniors. We had boys upstairs and girls downstairs. The teachers I remember were a Miss Hepple, Robinson, Lillian and Margaret Holmes. Miss Holmes was the headmistress. We had classes of around forty-five. The lessons included Maths, English, History, Geography, PE and sewing,

and we had to go to Brighton Avenue for cookery. We had outside toilets that froze in winter and you had to put your coat on the lid to go. I remember we really regarded our teachers with great respect. They could leave the class in charge of a prefect and the children did not misbehave, they just got on with their work.

Trudy Baister

Item cuckoo

When I was at Brighton Avenue school during the 1950s, a highlight of the year was going to the Town Hall in Gateshead to see the drama. We all piled into the double-decker buses and went to the Town Hall. It had lovely red seats and a stage. The plays always began with a lady dressed up in a fancy costume and a 'dames' hat, and she would be in bright colours. She would pop her head through the middle of the curtains and say; 'Item number one – CUCKOO' and every little play was announced in this way year after year. There was also a schools music festival every year, and all the Gateshead schools sang and took part.

Mrs A.M.

Jelly bags and black robes

We had to sit an eleven-plus exam in junior school, and if you passed you went to the Girl's Grammar, which was on Dryden Road, Low Fell. This was considered a very posh area to us Bensham folk and seemed a million miles away from home. You could catch the scholar's bus from Saltwell Road and this cost one penny. I remember the grey uniform; you had to wear a pinafore in the first year and there was a grey gabardine coat which nearly touched your ankles (room for growth our parents said). You also had to wear a pair of white knickers and then a pair of grey ones on top. The hats were either a knitted grey 'jelly-bag' or a grey felt thing. If a teacher or prefect caught you without your hat you were given detention. The same if you were found eating in uniform or going into a shop. Assemblies were every morning. When the headmistress, Miss Gillet, came flowing down the aisle in her black robes everyone had to stand up, and this applied whenever any teacher came into the room. You had to stand until given permission to sit.

Mrs A.M.

Teachers I remember

Miss Parker, the English teacher, was a firm favourite, and Miss Ramshaw, who taught Latin. She could have floored any Roman centurion but she had a great sense of humour. Woe betide anyone who crossed Miss Kilgour, the needlework teacher. Tales of life in the needlework room could merit an entire book of X-rated horror stories, from knicker elastic to threading up sewing machines. Did anyone ever wear those school-made bloomers? There was Mrs Lamb, the Geography teacher, and Miss Garvock, the P.E. teacher, who counted us all into showers despite our excuses of double pneumonia.

Mrs A.M.

Seven short years

Those long-suffering science teachers who watched their novices mix copper sulphate crystals and water year after year.

Then there was the carol service, a very much rehearsed, but well-loved yearly event, masterminded by the enthusiastic music department. I spent seven years of my life within those structured brick walls, and I think it fair to say that most of us loved being

part of this special traditional setting in Gateshead (all except for needlework class!)

Mrs A.M.

6d a day

The way the bairns used to be dressed. I've got some pictures of me starting school at five at Whitehall School. They wouldn't take you until you were five. We used to pay 6d a week each Monday morning. The people downstairs from us had four bairns and they used to go. We paid that for a canny bit of time.

Violet Wallace

Marmalade pudding

I stayed for school dinners on one or two occasions, but one day, when the food came, it was horrible. We thought that was bad but when the pudding came this was vile too. I was sure I had been poisoned. Now we weren't supposed to leave the school when we stayed for dinner, but I left to go to tell Granny Holmes that I'd been poisoned at school. The poor old soul wasn't too well, but she got her clothes on and took me back to school. She found Miss Weaver, the teacher on dinner duty, and we went up the fire escape to the canteen. There, my gran insisted upon knowing what it was I had been fed for pudding. It turned out it was Marmalade Pudding. I hated marmalade after that for years.

Audrey Stephenson

Hoy oot tactics

Another time, in Alexandra Road school, the caretaker's son got married, and the car came into the schoolyard. They did the usual things and eventually someone shouted

'Hoy canny man, hoy a ha'penny oot...'

I was small and at the back of the large crowd of children, and didn't really stand a chance of getting a coin, but this silver 6d came through all the legs and rolled right to me feet. I was thrilled.

Audrey Stephenson

She's a teecha

We had big classes then, but were not allowed to exceed fory-nine. I can remember frequently having forty-five plus.

When the children first started we would pin a name to them until, after about three days, we knew them all off by heart. I'm sure some children didn't see us as human. On one occasion, I overheard some children discussing letting me past on a tight path. One said, 'Let this woman past' to his friend. The other replied 'That's no woman, she's a teecha.'

Audrey Stephenson

Radiant Way

When I was at Prior school we were one of the first to use the Ladybird readers, this was after Janet and John had been dropped. I learnt on Radiant Way in the forties. We streamed them for the eleven plus then, and one of the tests was the reading test.

Richard Stephenson

Triple whammy

There was one child we all three taught at separate times of our careers. I had John Ellison as an infant, my husband Richard taught him as a junior, and finally dad taught him at his senior school.

Audrey Stephenson

Reading schemes

The reading scheme we had then was Dick and Dory. We didn't have Janet and John, although many did in the fifties.

Richard Stephenson

A star

Our star pupil in my time from Prior Street was Hayden Jenkins. He went from the boys Grammar to Oxford. We only had a handful ever get through to any university, never mind Oxford in the 1950s, this was exceptional at the time.

Richard Stephenson

Swimming

We took our classes from Prior Street through the streets to Mulgrave baths. When I first

An inside page from 'The Radiant Way'.

Radiant Way reading scheme was popular in the 1940s and 1950s.

Children from Redheugh, 1963. Richard Stephenson is the teacher on the left.

took a class they had to change in what was commonly referred to as 'cages'. This was simply a large lock-up area. When they were overlong, I would shout 'Hurry up girls or else I'll open the door on the cage,' this usually concentrated their minds. Later Mulgrave fitted individual changing rooms along the walls. There was also the slipper baths there. These were bathing facilities for those who had no bath inside their house. There was only bathing or swimming here, no laundry facilities, and it was the only place to go for a swim until Shipcote baths followed later in the 1950s.

We got the authority to provide buses to take the children from Chester Place school, especially if they were going further a field, for example Dunston baths.

I can't ever remember taking the children swimming from Redheugh school.

Richard Stephenson

Notable swimmers

Norman Sarsfield taught me to dive at Shipcote baths. He wouldn't waste his time with anyone he thought may not have it in them to be exceptional, and was always on the lookout for a potential star. I'm surprised he bothered with me, but I suppose I was reasonable diving off the high springboard at one time.

The other teachers that concentrated upon children becoming generally better all-round swimmers were Messrs. Webshaw and Wilkinson. They were still good coaches but Norman, as I said, was for those with special qualities. Norman can be credited in finding and nurturing Brian Phelps and Dorinda Fraser, both of whom represented England in the 1960s.

Audrey Stephenson

First teacher – Miss Pie

I was born on 23 December 1918. I lived, at first, in Dunsmuir Grove, and then Rectory Road. I went to Kelvin Grove School. One of the teachers I remember well was Miss Pie. She used to bang our heads together if anyone talked. We had slates and a slate pencil to write with then. There were about forty in the classes. Opposite our school was the Catholic school, Corpus Christi. We used to line up and throw snowballs at them in the winter from our yard.

Dorothy Dick

Form 1F, Gateshead Girl's Grammar school.

She can't go

Some had to pay to get into school. Me mam's mam was left a widow early and she started a shop. She then paid for her children to go to the Central school. My mam passed to go to the grammar, it was a lovely school the old grammar, it should have been a listed building. I can't understand them pulling it down. Well, me mam shone and she should have gone on to be a teacher, but me gran hadn't the money and anyway, the boys had to have what money there was. It was the same with her sister. When the head sent a letter to attend and discuss their future, me gran went up and said 'Oh no, she has to come home. She's the eldest girl and she has to help look after the house with me', and that was that. Me mam was bitter for a considerable time after this she told me.

Audrey Routledge

Black-shirts

There was a whisper set off at school that so and so was a 'black-shirt.' I think it was Mary Morris' father. It was a bit of a mystery to me, but I remember it sounded a bad thing to be.

Audrey Routledge

Fit babies

In the 'babies' school was Mrs Edwards. Oh, I remember her grip was like iron. If you were in the yard and linking up in a ring, and you were unfortunate enough to have to hold her hand, you would hate her very tight grip. The babies schoolyard was small and on a slope. If we needed space for anything then we would have to go down to the shuttles.

Miss Scollick wore long boots all the time, and occasionally took a fit. We all peered over her when this happened – fascination I suppose. We were a little frightened of her because of this. Miss Humble was the head of the babies' school.

Audrey Routledge

Settlement nursery

I went to the nursery at the Bensham Settlement. It was the first nursery school. Then I attended Brighton Avenue School. I remember my teacher was called Miss Tin. We wrote with a piece of slate on a slate board. Miss Tin was old and wore a long brown tunic. She was always kind to me. When I went into junior school, my first teacher was Miss

12.11.34.   <u>November</u>. by. J. Galsworthy .
Leaves from the elm trees flying —
   Summer to autumn flown —
   Out on the lawn is lying.
      Mulberry's golden gown.

Never a bird is singing
   Never a plant has bloom.
   Only. the fantails winging
      White on the windy gloom.

We can no more remember
   Perfume of rose or hay
   Far from this dark November.
      Beauty has passed away

Not till the. Spring recapture .
Joy as it flits along
   Shall we regain the rapture
   Either of scent or song .

      <u>Mr Colummy</u>.
Mr Colummy is out in his park.
   He and his tummy.
      Mr Colummy.
As soon as they see him the little dogs bark
oh ever so rummy.
      Is Mr Colummy. —

Mr Calummy is ros' with the lark;

Audrey Routledge was good at English and proud to show her work achievement from 1934.

Wishart. She was a horrible snob and hated us poor children with raggy clothes. Miss Featherstone was even worse. When anyone went to the clinic to have teeth out they were allowed to sit and be excused from lessons when they got back, but the poorer children, like me, just had to get on with it. She was very cruel to us poor ones.

Mary Davidson

First kindness

One Christmas I could not pay my party money, so I had to sit in the classroom on my own as the party was taking place. I remember Miss Hetherington. When we had cookery downstairs, I was allowed to cook for the teacher, as I could not pay my money and thus take the cooking home. Miss Dawson was the head teacher. She was a sergeant major type person, and we had to clean her great big clump shoes for her.

We would be given a half-day off every 24 May on Empire Day. We always marched into the hall and sang songs about our country then.

Mary Davidson

Scots kindness

I was at Brighton Avenue school until I left in 1939, when I was fourteen. I think Mr Dark was the headmaster. Teachers I can remember were Mrs Heslop, Miss Bent, Mr Hewitt, Mr Wales and Mr Bell. Mr Bell once gave me some boots because we couldn't afford any. I was good at football and played a lot, but I couldn't become a regular on the team because I didn't have football boots.

I recall having yet another major disappointment when I was chosen to go to school camp at Blackhall Rocks. My parents told the school it was out of the question, as we had no money. You can imagine my feelings when a kind Scottish lady gave me the two shillings to go. I remember thinking I was a millionaire. I brought a box of sweets back for the lady, the teachers and one for each of my family.

Robert Davidson

Miss Pigg

Miss Tate was my headmistress at Oswald House. Miss Moffatt lived in Airey Terrace. Another teacher was Miss Pigg. I seem to recall she went to Canada to marry, but it ended in divorce and she came back to Jarrow and eventually taught us. We would giggle at her name. There was a Mrs Edwards, and a Mrs Holliday who lived in a big house near to here (Low Fell), I believe it was Kellfield Avenue.

She came to our school from Kenton Lodge Teachers Training College. She was lovely. They all had lovely short skirts; we would die to have had garments like that. Mrs Holliday eventually replaced Miss Tate as headmistress.

Audrey Routledge

Wilde days

I started my school days in 1943 at Kelvin Grove School. It wasn't far to walk. I would go along Saltwell Road, then up Faraday Grove and into school. Apart from Kelvin Grove, the local schools then were Corpus Christi and Brighton Avenue.

My teacher was Miss Wilde in the infants, Miss Brogue in the juniors, and Mr Tait, and Mr Appleby in the senior school.

Ian Hampton

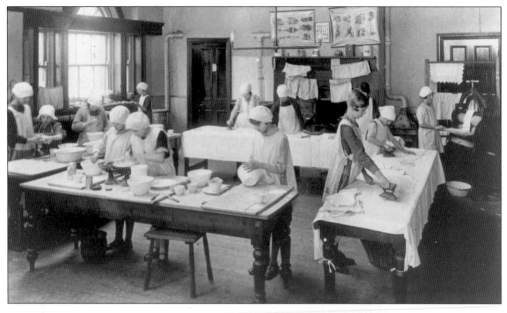

A domestic science room, typical of this area and elsewhere in the country, 1928. Trudy Baister well remembers having to go along from Kelvin Grove to Brighton Avenue School to do cookery, like these girls. (courtesy: Gateshead Central Library)

Last day decision

The day Miss Tate left, she met my mother and she said 'I've been clearing out my desk and I've got all your Audrey's essays, I just can't bare to throw them out.' I said to me mam, 'I wish she had given them all to me.' I was quite good at English.

Audrey Routledge

Plum pudding

Every year we did Christmas Carol and everyone wanted to be in it because you got a plum pudding. That was a real treat then. I was no actress; I was too shy,

Audrey Routledge

Commercial College

I enjoyed my school years and I stayed on and went to Commercial College. It was called the British Commercial College.

It had an office in the Theatre Royal building. We could go out onto the balcony in our lunchtimes, I loved doing that. I got a job in the Co-op in their offices soon afterwards.

Audrey Routledge

Craft

I was good at woodwork at school. My father was a craftsman and when I was little all his work was done on benches. We had a choice and could do metal or woodwork. I choose woodwork. We could do it for two years but I managed to stay on for a further year. I took after me dad see?

Ken Routledge

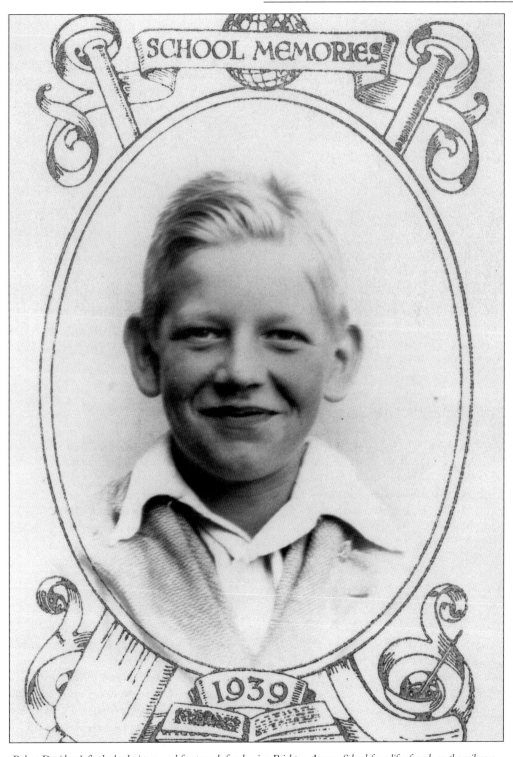

Robert Davidson's final school picture aged fourteen, before leaving Brighton Avenue School for a life of work on the railways.

Old boys

Most of my boyhood pals moved into Whickham from Bensham, and we still socialise together, but some have lost touch and sadly two or three have died. My childhood in Bensham was happy, even if the days weren't always so warm, especially in the severe winter of 1947. It was then I waited in a huge queue at the local merchants for two hours so I could collect a bag of sea-coal and haul it back home on a sledge. Some of my friends were in the same queue, and that day is fondly recalled whenever we get together. The following friends, who were all inter-dependent on each other, supported my formative years. Bob Johnson, Billy Gallon, Peter Hamilton, Billy Huntley, Norman Banham, Peter McCormack, John Tait, Alf Maddison, Frank Prevaz, Alan Simpson, Sid Dodds, Bob Moreland, Fatty Hindmarsh, Alan Johnson, Jimmy and Neville Chambers. The well-spoken and courteous Frizzell brothers, and last but not least, Fatty Fowler, who split my eye open with a brick – he was a rotten shot and was aiming for someone else.

Finally there were of course many members of the gentler sex in Bensham, but we didn't think of girls as human beings and playing doctors and nurses would have been completely alien to us – we were far too interested in football and railways!

Ian Hampton

School board man

I remember my daughter was off school one morning ill in the mid-fifties. She went back in the afternoon, but at about 2 p.m. there was a knock at the door and it was the school board man. I was horrified. The school then used to notify him instantly if anyone was missing. I got such a shock as I thought she hadn't turned up in the afternoon session. I said to him 'but she's already back at school, go and check if you want.' Talk about quick off the mark!

Mary Davidson

Toffee for all

When I was at school at Brighton Avenue there was a toffee factory on Liddell Terrace, near the school. At dinnertime we would walk around the back and watch the man stoking up the fires. He would sometimes throw us some toffees, and every Christmas they would also send boxes of toffees to the school. I think it was called Parkside Toffee factory, but I might be wrong. I also recall going to another factory near Saltwell Road with a basin and getting hot beetroot – delicious.

Mary Davidson

St Joan of Arc School

I remember starting St Joan of Arc Reg Charlton school from when I was seven years old in 1947. My dad Tommy Carrick had become school caretaker after my granda Edward retired. In the school hall they used to have dances on a weekend and that's where me mam and dad met and how I got the name Joan. My granda used to be the M.C. at those dances; some people still talk about them.

St Joan's was a bungalow type of school. It had a quadrangle all around so we could go from class to class without getting wet. At the time dad became caretaker, we were a family of six and then, in 1952, along came Kevin, so then we were seven. As a family we were always together, so after school we would stay behind and help mam and dad with small jobs and then all go home together. In the summer holidays the school would get a good old clean, mam and dad worked really hard and

Bensham Grove Nursery School children taken to sit at Bensham Station for a treat, to await and cheer past the brand new crack streamlined Silver Jubilee Express in 1936. (courtesy: Gateshead Central Library)

...and this is what they were waiting for! (seen clearing the King Edward VII Bridge to Bensham beyond), 1936. (courtesy: Bryce Greenfield Collection)

1948 class photo St Joan of Arc school. Maria Thompson is sixth from right in the second row.
Other names include Doreen Burton, Veronica Hopwood, Carol Dixon, Patricia O'Hagan, Peter Laidler, John
Creeby, Leo Dixon, Kathleen King, Eileen Mallet, Ina McLaren, Connie Riley and Veronica Vere.

everything was spotless. In those days we used to take sandwiches and lemonade and have a picnic in the schoolyard, summers were warm and we made our own amusements.

I remember mass being said in the school hall because we had no church. That hall was for everything. Mr Cahill was the parish priest, he had a house in Tynedale Terrace where the front room was converted into a small chapel and morning mass was said.

Around 1953, the Holy Rosary church was built. I remember the processions on holy days. We would walk around the school yard singing hymns as loud as we could and the people from over the road would come over to listen and watch us in our white dresses.

St Joan's had a great netball team and won the shield many times. Miss Swallow was very proud of us and also our dancing exploits too. I loved sports. In my last year we had our sports day and I thought I'd win the cup, but another girl won, nevertheless I loved every minute of my time there.

Joan Wharton